Praise for Through the Eyes of a Tiger

Through the Eyes of a Tiger is a worthy addition to the literature of the AVG Flying Tigers. John Donovan was not one of the lucky ones who came home to tell his story. Author Susan Clotfelter Jimison speaks for him here, with much of the story told in Donovan's own words, via the detailed letters he sent back to his family. Combined with the author's useful notes, the book becomes a chronicle of the everyday life of the AVG pilots during the war's early days in Burma and China. This interesting, often exciting account is possibly the best picture we have of the human side of the Flying Tigers' war.

—**Bob Bergin**, author of *Tracking the Tiger: Flying Tiger, OSS and Free Thai Operations in World War II Thailand, When Tigers Fly* and many others

The famous Flying Tigers of World War Two were a group of American aviators sponsored by the U.S. government who fought with the Chinese government of Chang Kai-shek against the Imperial Japanese Army that had invaded China in the late 1930s. The "Tigers," whose planes' noses were decorated with shark eyes and teeth, were lauded throughout the world for their derring-do and masterful flying abilities, fighting Japanese pilots. In this absorbing story Susan Jimison painstakingly and faithfully reconstructs the career of her cousin, John Tyler Donovan, a pilot who was killed while attacking a Japanese-held airfield near Hanoi, Vietnam. Using Donovan's private letters to his family, Jimison forms a haunting tale of courage, patriotism, and tragedy that will keep the reader on the edge throughout this fascinating book.

—**Winston Groom**, NYT bestselling author of *Forrest Gump*

Susan Clotfelter Jimison has become one of my favorite authors. First with the moving story of her brother in *Dear Mark* and now *Through the Eyes of a Tiger,* the moving story of World War II aviator John Donovan. Utilizing real life letters with a healthy dose of expert storytelling Susan weaves another important story of war and family and heroes and prices paid. Thank you Susan for introducing Mark Clotfelter and John Donovan into our lives. May we never forget them and the many like them. American Boys who rose above themselves to give ALL they had for freedom.

—**Joseph S. Bonsall**, Oak Ridge Boy and author of *G.I. Joe and Lillie*

THROUGH THE EYES OF A
TIGER
THE JOHN DONOVAN STORY

Herb and Sue Rusk
6167 Brookside Ln
Hoschton, GA 30548-8200

THROUGH THE EYES OF A TIGER

THE JOHN DONOVAN STORY

BY SUSAN CLOTFELTER JIMISON

Herb, Cousin Herb -
what a small world.
Hope you enjoy John's story -
Susan Clotfelter Jimison

Deeds Publishing | Atlanta

Published by Deeds Publishing in Athens, GA
www.deedspublishing.com

Printed in The United States of America

Library of Congress Cataloging-in-Publications Data is available upon request.

ISBN 978-1-941165-88-1

Books are available in quantity for promotional or premium use. For information, email info@deedspublishing.com.

First Edition, 2015

10 9 8 7 6 5 4 3 2 1

Dedicated to James Donovan
1920-2013

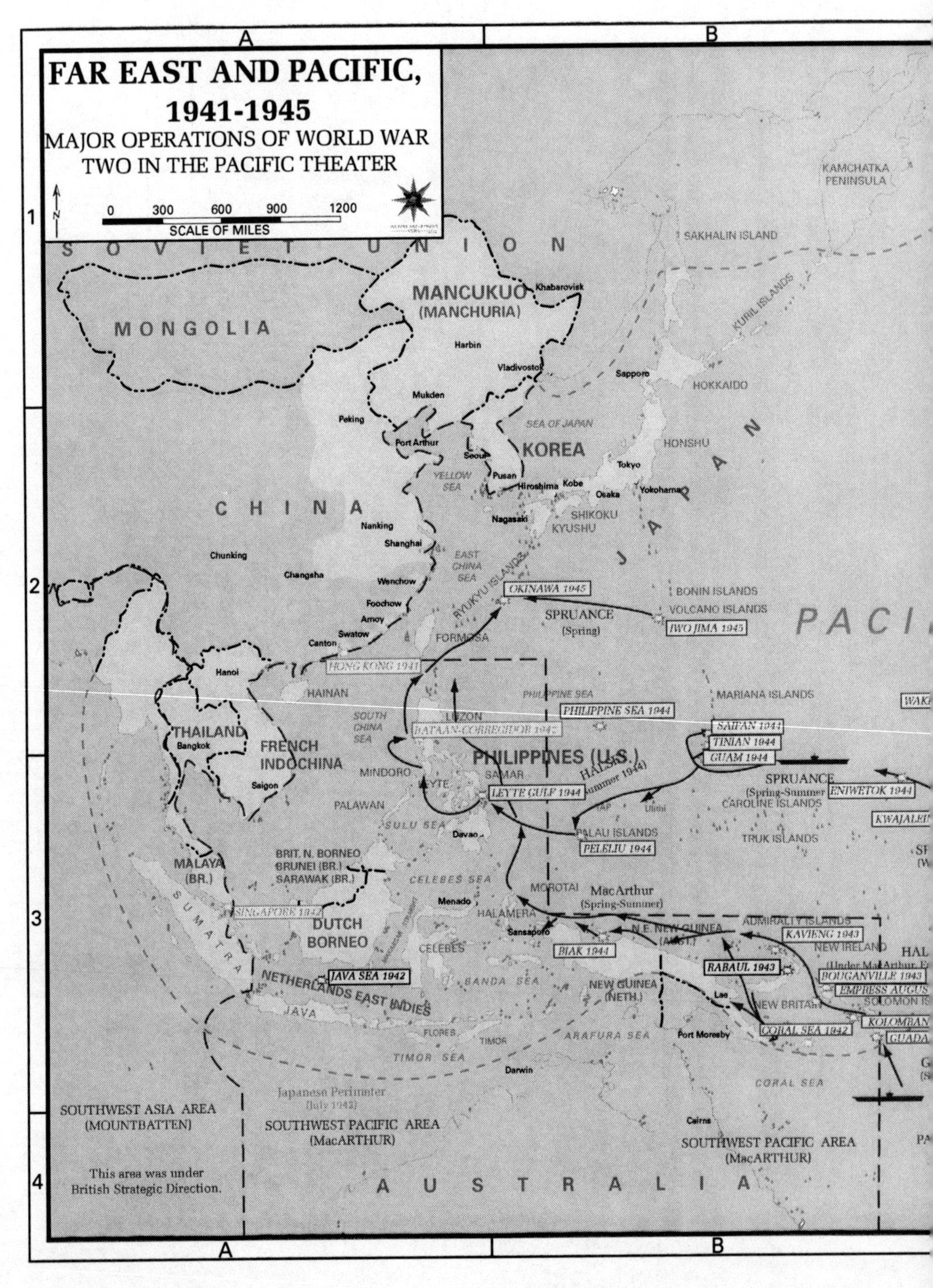
FAR EAST AND PACIFIC, 1941-1945
MAJOR OPERATIONS OF WORLD WAR TWO IN THE PACIFIC THEATER
SCALE OF MILES
0 300 600 900 1200
SOVIET UNION
MONGOLIA
MANCUKUO (MANCHURIA)
KOREA
CHINA
JAPAN
PACI
KAMCHATKA PENINSULA
SAKHALIN ISLAND
KURIL ISLANDS
HOKKAIDO
HONSHU
SHIKOKU
KYUSHU
SEA OF JAPAN
YELLOW SEA
EAST CHINA SEA
SOUTH CHINA SEA
PHILIPPINE SEA
SULU SEA
CELEBES SEA
BANDA SEA
ARAFURA SEA
TIMOR SEA
CORAL SEA
OKINAWA 1945
IWO JIMA 1945
HONG KONG 1941
BATAAN-CORREGIDOR 1942
PHILIPPINE SEA 1944
SAIPAN 1944
TINIAN 1944
GUAM 1944
LEYTE GULF 1944
PELELIU 1944
ENIWETOK 1944
SINGAPORE 1942
JAVA SEA 1942
BIAK 1944
RABAUL 1943
KAVIENG 1943
BOUGANVILLE 1943
CORAL SEA 1942
SPRUANCE (Spring)
SPRUANCE (Spring-Summer)
HALSEY (Summer 1944)
MacArthur (Spring-Summer)
PHILIPPINES (U.S.)
THAILAND
FRENCH INDOCHINA
MALAYA (BR.)
BRIT. N. BORNEO
BRUNEI (BR.)
SARAWAK (BR.)
DUTCH BORNEO
NETHERLANDS EAST INDIES
SUMATRA
JAVA
CELEBES
NEW GUINEA (NETH.)
N.E. NEW GUINEA (AUST.)
NEW BRITAIN
NEW IRELAND
ADMIRALTY ISLANDS
AUSTRALIA
Japanese Perimeter (July 1942)
SOUTHWEST ASIA AREA (MOUNTBATTEN)
This area was under British Strategic Direction.
SOUTHWEST PACIFIC AREA (MacARTHUR)
Khabarovsk
Harbin
Vladivostok
Mukden
Peking
Port Arthur
Seoul
Pusan
Hiroshima
Kobe
Osaka
Tokyo
Yokohama
Sapporo
Nagasaki
Nanking
Shanghai
Chunking
Changsha
Wenchow
Foochow
Amoy
Swatow
Canton
Hanoi
Bangkok
Saigon
HAINAN
FORMOSA
LUZON
MINDORO
SAMAR
LEYTE
PALAWAN
Davao
Menado
MOROTAI
HALMAHERA
Sansapor
RYUKYU ISLANDS
BONIN ISLANDS
VOLCANO ISLANDS
MARIANA ISLANDS
CAROLINE ISLANDS
PALAU ISLANDS
TRUK ISLANDS
Ulithi
Yap
Lae
Port Moresby
FLORES
TIMOR
Darwin
Cairns

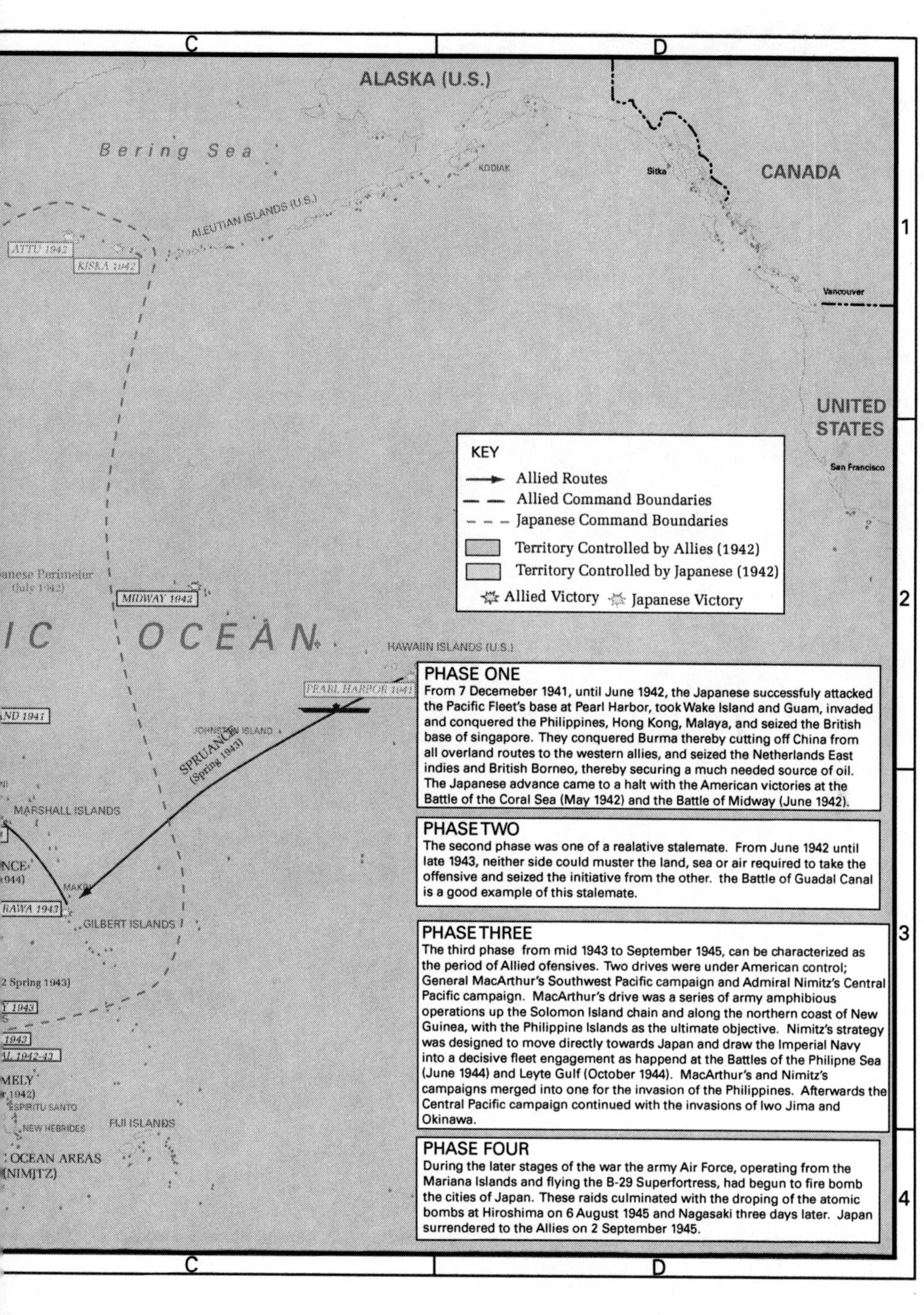

C
D
ALASKA (U.S.)
Bering Sea
KODIAK
Sitka
CANADA
ALEUTIAN ISLANDS (U.S.)
ATTU 1942
KISKA 1942
Vancouver
UNITED STATES
San Francisco
KEY
Allied Routes
Allied Command Boundaries
Japanese Command Boundaries
Territory Controlled by Allies (1942)
Territory Controlled by Japanese (1942)
Allied Victory
Japanese Victory
MIDWAY 1942
OCEAN
HAWAIIN ISLANDS (U.S.)
PEARL HARBOR 1941
JOHNSTON ISLAND
SPRUANCE (Spring 1943)
MARSHALL ISLANDS
GILBERT ISLANDS
ESPIRITU SANTO
NEW HEBRIDES
FIJI ISLANDS
1
2
3
4
PHASE ONE
From 7 Decemeber 1941, until June 1942, the Japanese successfuly attacked the Pacific Fleet's base at Pearl Harbor, took Wake Island and Guam, invaded and conquered the Philippines, Hong Kong, Malaya, and seized the British base of singapore. They conquered Burma thereby cutting off China from all overland routes to the western allies, and seized the Netherlands East indies and British Borneo, thereby securing a much needed source of oil. The Japanese advance came to a halt with the American victories at the Battle of the Coral Sea (May 1942) and the Battle of Midway (June 1942).
PHASE TWO
The second phase was one of a realative stalemate. From June 1942 until late 1943, neither side could muster the land, sea or air required to take the offensive and seized the initiative from the other. the Battle of Guadal Canal is a good example of this stalemate.
PHASE THREE
The third phase from mid 1943 to September 1945, can be characterized as the period of Allied ofensives. Two drives were under American control; General MacArthur's Southwest Pacific campaign and Admiral Nimitz's Central Pacific campaign. MacArthur's drive was a series of army amphibious operations up the Solomon Island chain and along the northern coast of New Guinea, with the Philippine Islands as the ultimate objective. Nimitz's strategy was designed to move directly towards Japan and draw the Imperial Navy into a decisive fleet engagement as happend at the Battles of the Philipne Sea (June 1944) and Leyte Gulf (October 1944). MacArthur's and Nimitz's campaigns merged into one for the invasion of the Philippines. Afterwards the Central Pacific campaign continued with the invasions of Iwo Jima and Okinawa.
PHASE FOUR
During the later stages of the war the army Air Force, operating from the Mariana Islands and flying the B-29 Superfortress, had begun to fire bomb the cities of Japan. These raids culminated with the droping of the atomic bombs at Hiroshima on 6 August 1945 and Nagasaki three days later. Japan surrendered to the Allies on 2 September 1945.

CONTENTS

DISCLAIMER

John Donovan's letters reflect the language, stereotypes, and societal norms of his era, although they have been retyped for legibility. Words typical of 1941, such as to-night and to-morrow, have been updated for ease of reading. The names of some cities and countries were changed to reflect 21st century terms. Other than those changes, letters remain exactly as John wrote them, including some that appear unfinished. No letter was omitted from his story.

"... There are no bounds of place or time to the memory of those who die for love of men. As China grieves with you in your great sorrow, she is also proud to claim part in preserving the record of his fair name."

—Madame Chiang Kai-shek

PREFACE

"I can assure you that he died with his face to the enemy and with his machine guns flaming a challenge to the enemies of our country."
—General Claire Chennault, July 22, 1942

In 1941, as the second Sino-Japanese War raged in Asia, the Chinese people desperately needed help repelling the ever-powerful Japanese military. Japan had invaded and seized Manchuria—the entire Northeastern area of China—then celebrated a bloody victory in Shanghai. Soon after, upon orders from their superiors, the Japanese army looted and murdered half the 600,000 citizens of Nanking. Entire families were raped and then slaughtered. Nanking was left in ruins following the savage attacks and took decades to rebuild.

All of these atrocities were committed for the sake of seizing land under Japan's Tanaka plan, "The Dream of World Empire," a blueprint for world conquest. Japan was 1/20th the size of China—and hungered for China's vast land and natural resources. Despite the size disparity, China's military was far inferior and battle-weary after ten years of Japan's relentless pounding. The situation was dire, and the leaders of China sought military training and support from the United States' government.

War was under way in many parts of the world but had not yet come to the shores of the United States. Secretary of the Treasury, Henry

Morgenthau, arranged for a loan to China for planes and looked forward to the possibility of U.S. planes operating under the Chinese Air Force that would bomb Japan—the President agreed. Because the U.S. had not yet entered the war, it was critical to maintain the United States' position of neutrality. In an unprecedented move, President Franklin Delano Roosevelt authorized recruitment of some of the military's finest pilots and mechanics to assist the Chinese government as "civilian contract workers." In this agreement, the recruits were required to resign from their service branch, then after completing their year-long overseas commitment, they would be reinstated to their previous rank and position.

Unheard of before and since.

One hundred pilots took advantage of this opportunity. Some wanted to gain combat experience, some wanted the lucrative contract (three times that of military pay)—but all went for the adventure. This small band of brothers became known as "The Flying Tigers." Officially, they were the American Volunteer Group, led by World War I aviator General Claire Chennault.

In 1942, reports of their heroics traversed the Pacific Ocean, and America couldn't get enough. John Wayne starred in the blockbuster movie Flying Tigers. They became legendary, both in truth and in fiction. Some of the Tigers even penned their memoirs after their return.

Despite their early celebrity, their role, their heroics, and their lives have since faded into the annals of American history.

However, 8,000 miles away, in China—they continue to be remembered and honored. In addition to existing museums honoring the Flying Tigers in Kunming and Changsha, a new museum in Guilin, Heritage Park, broke ground in 2011 and is now open. The Chinese have not forgotten who came to their aid when the Japanese were hell-bent to annihilate them. To the Chinese, they were—and still are—heroes.

This is the story of one of those heroes, John Tyler Donovan, a Flying Tiger—and my first cousin once removed. When I read the fascinating, detailed letters he wrote to his family, it was clear to me he intended them to be shared with a wider audience. In these well-crafted historical gems, he reveals his innermost thoughts, his sense of adventure, hopes for the future, and perhaps a premonition of his own death. I'm grateful to his brother, James, who had the foresight to preserve these letters for future generations.

From the first letter I found in my grandmother's scrapbook to the archived letters and photographs I tracked down at the National Naval Aviation Museum—my cousin's life began to unfold.

I'm telling John's story because he never had the chance.

INTRODUCTION: BIRTH OF THE AVG

Madame Chiang, wife of the leader of China, Generalissimo Chiang Kai-shek, had an American education. She graduated from Wellesley College with a Bachelor's Degree in English Literature in 1917 at the age of 19. She was also a recipient of the Durant Scholar, one of the highest academic honors conferred by the college. Immediately following graduation, Mayling Soong (Madame Chiang's maiden name) returned to China after living in New England for over five years. Mayling and Chiang were married in 1927.

In the early stages of the Sino-Japanese War, Time magazine named Chiang Kai-shek and Mayling as "Man and Wife of the Year" in 1937. In the article, Chiang told the reporter: "Tell America to have complete confidence in us. The tide of battle is turning and eventually victory will be ours!" But China was being pummeled by Japan, and they needed help.

Mayling returned to the United States in 1937 and negotiated a commitment from retired Army aviator Colonel Claire Chennault to come to China and train the pilots. Based on his aviation skills and experience, she felt certain he would get the Chinese Air Force combat-ready. His World War I pursuit tactics and precision flying were well known throughout the aviation community. A predecessor to the Air Force acrobatics of The Thunderbirds, "The Three Men on a Flying Trapeze" demonstrated speed and precision flying led by Col. Chennault.

They performed in more than 50 air shows across the country. Chennault believed teamwork was the reason for their success. He took great pride in his reputation as a superb pilot. He did, however, butt heads with almost every superior in the military.

Upon his retirement from the Army, Chennault had many job opportunities. He had been offered a position as a test pilot/salesman with Curtiss-Wright Aircraft. Russia even wooed him with gifts and an offer of a lucrative contract to come to Russia and help build a paratroops division in their army. China offered him a position to put all of his combat aviation knowledge to use—and train its Air Force. Chennault had the need to achieve, to accomplish. He felt that his pursuit tactics that were rejected by the U.S. military would be successful in China and would prove he had been right all along.

In 1940, Chennault, T. V. Soong (Madame's brother and Minister of Foreign Affairs), Nelson T. Johnson, U.S. Ambassador to China, met with Generalissimo Chiang Kai-shek, who feared the collapse of China. Russia was withdrawing its support from China. The group agreed it was time to ask for aid from the U.S.

Chennault and Soong traveled to Washington, D.C., following the unprecedented 3rd term reelection of President Roosevelt to seek help from the United States. It was a simple premise: to successfully fend off the Japanese, they needed more planes and experienced pilots.

This meeting was the birth of The American Volunteer Group and the secret that facilitated that birth.

It was China's responsibility to obtain funds for the planes and armament. Central Aircraft Manufacturing Company's responsibility was to recruit pilots and ground crew. And it was Chennault's responsibility to lead the newly-recruited personnel in combat against the Japanese.

1. THE STORY BEGINS

John Jr., the first child of Stella and John Boston Donovan, was born April 30, 1915. Life was simple on Herron Street in Montgomery, Alabama, back in those days. Two years later, sister Mary Ellen was born, then brother James in 1920. Stella stayed home with her little ones, and their father worked as a policeman when the children were young.

Their simple Southern life became complicated during John Jr.'s high school years when John Sr. suffered a serious mental breakdown at the age of 52. Stella lovingly took care of her husband as best she could for a few years until it became apparent that he was never going to recover. Doctors encouraged institutional care at Bryce Hospital, two hours away in Tuscaloosa. It was the closest residential facility, enabling the family to visit on weekends.

As the eldest child, this tragedy was no doubt the foundation of John Jr.'s incredible sense of responsibility to his family. That same sense of responsibility drove him to excel at everything he set his mind to. From the debate team to Eagle Scouts to the ROTC program—John was a leader on his way to success.

Stella, head of the household now, worked as a clerk at Montgomery Fair department store. In winter, when darkness fell early, the boys would walk down to Bibb Street to accompany her home at the end of her shift. Mary Ellen helped out with the cooking. John delivered newspapers on his bicycle. Even with the remaining family members pitching in, money was tight.

"At times it was hard going to Sunday school because we didn't have a nickel to put in the collection plate, and dues were also a nickel for scouts. Sometimes it seemed easier to stay home than to go to scouts without a nickel." James told me during a 2009 visit.

John graduated from Sidney Lanier High School with big ideas in the height of the Great Depression. In 1933, with only ten dollars in his pocket and his mother's blessing, he hitchhiked to Chicago to see the World's Fair he had read so much about and to attend George Williams College. Upon arrival, he found work and a room at the YMCA Hotel on Wabash Avenue. Not only was John adventurous and studious, he was also an employee with a great work ethic. He often sent home cash neatly tucked inside letters to his mother.

Hard work was balanced with dating, dancing, and Alpha Omicron Alpha fraternity activities. His YMCA job paid for his education, room and board, and incidentals.

After completing his sophomore year, John moved back to Montgomery and decided to attend the University of Alabama. Going to school in Tuscaloosa afforded him more opportunity to visit his father.

Yet, only a year later, wanderlust pulled him to the West Coast. John, now 24 years old, graduated from the University of Southern California with a Bachelor of Science in Public Administration.

Immediately following his graduation, John enrolled at Loyola University, in Los Angeles, to study Law. However, not long after the semester began, he enlisted in the United States Navy.

On October 16, John reported for active duty in California. Following his initial military training, John was accepted into the flying program. After a somewhat hazardous road trip to Pensacola Naval Air Station with a fellow Navy cadet, he began flight training in January of 1940.

Here is where John's letters begin and tell his story best. Through his eyes, in his words, and with his photographs—his journey begins.

In this letter home to his folks, John reveals the horrible weather he encountered driving from the Navy base in California to the Florida panhandle. The amount of snowfall in Louisiana they encountered that week still holds the record—8.2 inches, as well as the greatest number of hours below freezing—116 hours. All this in a car without a heater.

As usual, John assures the family he is well and eager to get on with his training. He marvels at the base food and mentions how several cadets have "washed out" of training there.

Now only 170 miles from Montgomery, John plans a trip home as soon as he is scheduled off for a long weekend.

U.S. Naval Air Station
Pensacola, Florida
January 28, 1940

Dear Folks,

Arrived here last night (Saturday) about 8:30 p.m. after a rather hazardous trip.

As you know, we left Los Angeles about 3 p.m. Tuesday, Jan. 23. When we left California and got into Arizona, we ran into freezing temperatures. In the western part of New Mexico we began to encounter snow. All through the 7 or 8 hundred miles through the state of Texas there was snow and the temperature was about zero.

We hoped that as we approached the Deep South it would be warmer; instead, it was colder and the snow deeper.

The roads in Louisiana were terrible. It was almost impossible to tell where the road was. Snow was three feet thick in some places, and since we did not have a heater in the car, we nearly froze. Boy, after the sun went down, the temperature dropped like a rock.

About the worst part of the trip was from Shreveport to Vicksburg. Cars were piled up in the ditch on both sides of the road about every mile. The night we spent in Vicksburg, the temperature dropped to 6° below zero.

Realizing it would be impossible to go home, we cut down south after we got to Jackson and fortunately we ran out of the snow when we approached Gulfport. It was still cold, but the roads were clear. We found out that if we had followed the southern route from L.A., the roads were clear all the way.

People in Mobile were complaining about the cold, but they don't realize how much luckier they are than the people living 2 or 3 hundred miles farther north.

No doubt you folks have an inkling of what I'm talking about. Some fellows here said they had been through Birmingham, and there was plenty of snow there.

How about it, did it snow in Montgomery? How have you folks fared during this cold spell?

I'm sorry that I didn't get to come home because it seems that the first month here they keep us in pretty close, and we do everything but fly. The only time we see airplanes is when they fly overhead.

We have the toughest physical exam in a week. Two of the fellows from Long Beach base were sent back last week and another is slated to go this week on account of his eyes. The worry of all the cadets is whether they are going to "wash out." There are a million ways of "washing out." The first two weeks they throw things at you fast as a machine gun.

However, it's a swell place. All the fellows are swell and of the highest caliber you can find anywhere.

The buildings and equipment are new. As yet, however, I have not seen the base in its entirety.

Of course, the first chance I have, I will come home. After the first two weeks, I understand we are off from 4:00 p.m. Friday to 10:45 p.m. Sunday.

The food is swell. For breakfast we had fresh donuts (boy, were they good), eggs cooked any way, toast, any kind of cereal, bacon, milk, coffee, grapefruit. Now, it is lunch time and I'm not hungry at all.

We have already had some equipment issued, and tomorrow that is what we do all day long. We have about 8 uniforms that we wear on different occasions.

I have lots to do today so I had better get squared away. Wanted to let you know that I arrived here OK and everything is swell. Be sure to write and tell me about things at home.

My address here is:

Cadet John T. Donovan

Wing #1

Naval Air Station

Pensacola, Florida

Love,

John, Jr.

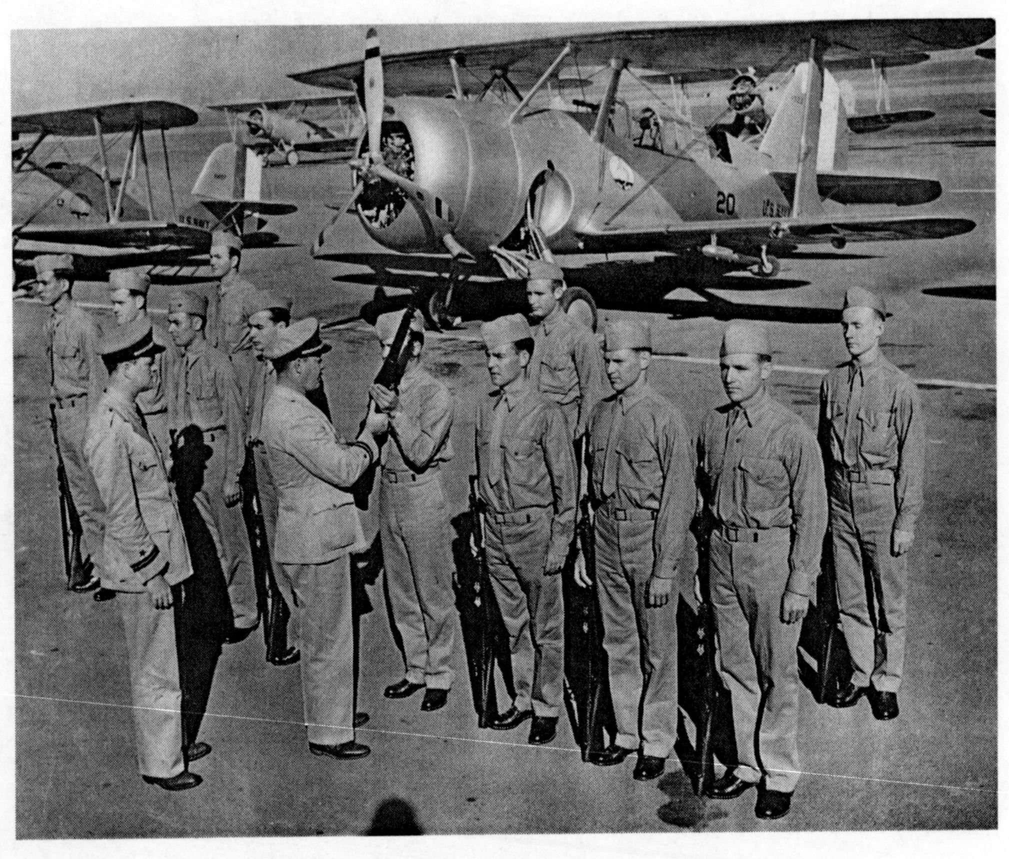

Pensacola Naval Air Station, Florida (John is back row-center)
National Naval Aviation Museum collection

2. MOTHER'S DAY

In this letter John writes of his gratitude to his mother for being such a profound influence on his life. With his father institutionalized, Stella had carried the uncommon burden of being a single mother in the '30s.

A favorite story James told me about their mother was when hobos would hop off the trains and come to their back door. Stella always found something to give them to eat—no matter how poor she was—always showing kindness and compassion.

Again, the pressure to succeed in his training is clear when he mentions the 20- and 30-hour check-rides in the aircraft. Check rides—flying with an instructor pilot after completing a set number of training hours, and written tests are frequent for the new pilots. Some pilots don't make it and "wash-out." He doesn't dwell on it. Instead, he urges Stella to buy a new hat so she can visit Pensacola. Perhaps he even tucked money in the envelope for the hat.

10 May 1940

Dearest Mother,

Every day is Mother's Day as far as I'm concerned. You

have done so much for me that I know I cannot ever repay the debt. You have been the strongest influence in my life, and I'm glad that that influence was good influence.

I do not adore you as a far-away creature with hands folded and settled in sweet repose. Sweet you are, but I know you as the best-dispositioned person I have ever known. While I slept in bed you were up in the cold starting a fire, and when I got up when the kitchen was warm, never was I met with a glum and sour greeting. Instead you were and are always cheerful. This virtue I cannot lay claim to. You are a wise, practical, good-natured, loving mother–and I lay tribute to your feet for being the best mother a fellow could have. I was certainly lucky to get you for a mother–for I'm quite sure no one else I could love quite so much.

Today I got the "up" that I needed so badly and believe I passed Plotting Board & Voice procedure exams ok.

Now I start flying NS's–a little different airplane. My next check is the 33-hour check that sends so many boys home. It consists mostly of stunts–but in addition you have pylons and small fields–this time Clay Pits is the small field (it's about the size of a pocket handkerchief). It seems smaller than that from the air. The stunts I will have to learn to perfection are: loops, wingovers, Immelmann's, snap rolls, splits, cartwheels, and falling leaf. Five fellows from our class go home on account of the 20-hour check, which I got by, by the skin of my teeth. One of the fellows was Taylor who trained with me in Long Beach.

It seems almost certain that we will go back to the year's course soon–that will bring more pitfalls.

Now I don't want you to not visit down here because you don't have a new hat. Therefore, when you have the chance, please get one so you can come down for a visit around June 1st.

Love,

John, Jr.

We have been moved to new quarters:

Cadet J.T. Donovan

Platoon 18 Naval Air Station

Pensacola, Florida

Cadet Donovan on the airfield in Pensacola, Florida, in full flying gear, including a Gosport Tube. The Gosport Tube was invented by Robert Raymond Smith-Barry in 1917 at The School of Special Flying in Gosport, England. The voice tube was used by instructor pilots in military aviation to give directions to the student pilot. The instructor would talk—the student listened: one-way communication only.

Photo courtesy of Kelleen Donovan Thornock

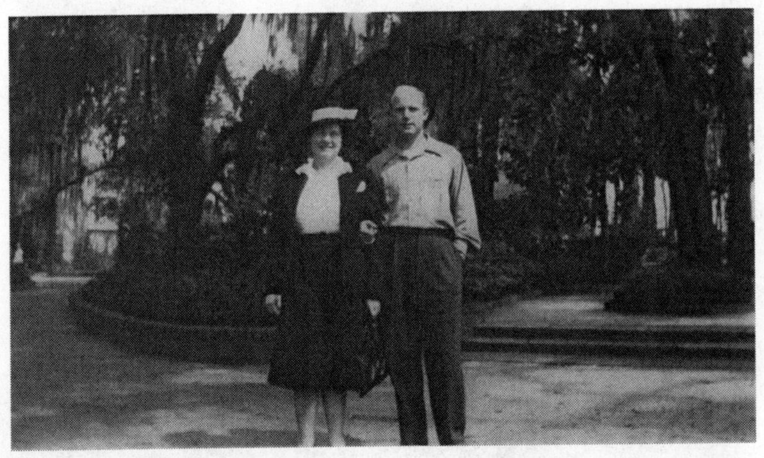

Mary Stella and John Donovan in Pensacola, Florida

Photo courtesy of Pat Donovan Hope

3. FDR'S SECRET

Revealed in the following declassified documents, President Roosevelt secretly authorized recruitment of military pilots and crew to aid the Chinese in their fight against Japan. Recruiting by Central Aircraft Manufacturing Company, CAMCO, began in March of 1941 at numerous bases across the United States. The recruits would leave their positions to "take employment with Central Aircraft Manufacturing Company" and would receive an honorable discharge upon completion of their year-long contract.

John, Greg "Pappy" Boyington, and Richard "Dick" Rossi, among others, attended the recruiting meeting August 1941 at the San Carlos Hotel on Palafox Street in Pensacola. During the meeting they were informed the monthly salaries were $750 for squadron commander, $600 for wingman, and $350-400 for ground crew. Pilots would receive an additional $500 for every Japanese plane they shot down. These were handsome wages in 1941. After surviving the Great Depression, the opportunity being offered was the chance of a lifetime: travel, adventure, and the opportunity to put some money in the bank.

Following the meeting, so many had signed up to go to China the base commander was furious at the thought of losing that number of instructor pilots. He ripped the list in half. Alphabetically, Rossi was not on the "right" side of the rip. Rossi went back to the recruiter and reapplied—not wanting to miss out on the grand adventure. He made it the second time.

When the resignations began, disgruntled commanders from across the country were all directed to call Washington, which quickly paved the way for a smooth transition. Discharge papers revealed they were released "for the convenience of the government." When the press got wind they jumped on it. But when they questioned the State Department, of course, no one would corroborate the story.

In only one month, this Pensacola group of military pilots-turned-mercenaries would be the last bunch of the First American Volunteer Group to board a ship for Burma.

Ironically, the contract they signed with CAMCO never mentioned combat or bonus—it didn't even mention flying.

In reply address not the signer of this letter, but Bureau of Navigation, Navy Department, Washington, D. C.

Refer to No. Nav-61-IBM

NAVY DEPARTMENT

BUREAU OF NAVIGATION

WASHINGTON, D. C.

August 8, 1941.

S E C R E T

MEMORANDUM FOR THE CHIEF OF THE BUREAU OF NAVIGATION:

SUBJECT: Enlisted Personnel - discharge of for China.

Sometime about the close of May, I was called in conference with Captain Shafroth (Naval Reserve Division), Captain Good (Central Division), Commander Lynch (Naval Reserve Division), Mr. Leighton, U.S. Naval Academy Class of '13, and one or two other civilians (ex-Army).

We were told that the Secretary of the Navy had directed that a certain number of Reserve Officers and an undetermined number of enlisted men who desired it should be separated from the service for employment in China to help the Chinese Government with their aircraft.

So far as enlisted personnel were concerned, it was agreed that:

(a) The civilians would be given necessary authority to interview officers and enlisted men in various aeronautical units of the Navy.

(b) At the expiration of their service in China, enlisted personnel would be permitted to reenlist in the regular Navy. Enlisted men consulted could be orally informed of this promise. The question was brought up as to what could be done for men who were killed in China, and it was agreed that their families could receive no benefits from the Government. It was not definitely settled, but my understanding was that the Chief of Bureau would be asked to recommend to the Secretary of the Navy that men, who returned and desired it, would be permitted to reenlist regardless of their physical condition. They would then be allowed to serve until they had sufficient time in service to retire.

(c) All requests for discharge should state that men desired to take employment with the Central Aircraft Manufacturing Co., which would signify that they were going to China.

(d) The matter was secret.

Forty-five men have been discharged to date for this project.

H M Briggs

H. M. BRIGGS.

(A)

National Archives, College Park, Maryland

WASHINGTON

September 30, 1941

MEMORANDUM FOR THE SECRETARY OF THE NAVY:

I have been informed that the Chinese Government has hired 100 pilots and 181 ground personnel to man and service 100 P-40's. In the next few months we are delivering to China 269 pursuit planes and 66 bombers. The Chinese pilot training program here will not begin to turn out well-trained pilots until next summer. In the interim, therefore, I think we should facilitate the hiring by the Chinese Government of further volunteer pilots here. I suggest, therefore, that beginning in January, you should accept the resignations of additional pilots and ground personnel as care to accept employment in China, up to a limit of 100 pilots and a proportional number of ground personnel. I am directing Mr. Lauchlin Currie to see that representatives of China carry out the hiring program with the minimum of inconvenience to the Navy and also to see that no more are hired than are necessary.

Franklin D. Roosevelt

SECRETARY'S OFFICE
RECEIVED
OCT 4 - 1941
NAVY DEPARTMENT

Courtesy of Alan Armstrong, Author of Preemptive Strike

4. COLD FEET

John purchased a new portable Remington typewriter, and this is the first of many typed letters home. While in San Francisco, where he will embark, John explains what it will cost to send mail to him, how he wants his mother to manage his wages, and his contact information. Not having children of his own, he also reminds Stella to deposit a little money in an account for his infant nephew, Wayne.

John includes family friend Sybil's address. Sybil and Stella planned to share news they received from John. Instead of writing multiple letters, sometimes John used carbon paper so he was able to send the same letter to two people.

For the first time since signing his contract with CAMCO, as he awaits departure, John mentions "getting the cold feet."

Although John was headed off to war, the United States was determined to maintain neutrality; life carried on as usual in the States. However, life was anything but normal in many parts of the world. In addition to Japan's continued attacks on China, under Adolf Hitler's Nazi regime, Germany was bombing Ireland and Great Britain was at war with Germany. Hitler's systematic euthanasia of the mentally ill and the disabled was shocking the world.

San Francisco
23 September 1941

Dearest Folks,

We sail tomorrow.

How do you like my new typewriter—portable—vellee good.

If the picture "Kukan" comes to town, be sure to see it. It tells a graphic story of China in Technicolor.

Regular first-class mail to Rangoon is 5¢ for the first ounce, 3¢ for an additional ounce. Delivery takes from 23 to 26 days from San Francisco.

Air-Mail is 70¢ for ½ ounce and takes 14 days from San Francisco. Parcel Post is 62¢ for the first pound and 90¢ up to 3 pounds.

Use regular mail unless something comes up.

It will be about six weeks before we reach Rangoon. I will write en route. Inasmuch as we do not know what ports we are stopping at, send my mail to Rangoon. I hope to have some there for me when I arrive.

My address again:

John Tyler Donovan

Central Aircraft Manufacturing Company

Rangoon, Burma

Sybil's address is:
Miss Sybil Simpson
Evangeline Residence
1305 W. 6th Street
Los Angeles, California

The last that I heard from her was she had a job and she was going to school. When our boat was delayed the last time, she came up and spent the weekend here and enjoyed it very much. She is agog about all of California, and you probably couldn't run her out with a gun.

I have my allotment changed to send me $75 per month instead of $50. The balance of my salary should be in the bank by the 15th of the month, inasmuch as it is due on the 1st. If these deposits are not made regularly please let me know.

Don't forget to deposit 5 or 10 dollars each month to Wayne's bank account.

Because I had to make a quick cash sale of my car to a used car dealer, I was only paid $290 for it. It has a 'Blue Book' value of $350. Please let me know if you receive the duplicate deposit slip from the Southern California Building and Loan Association as requested in the carbon copy enclosed. The $60 in cash deposited is a major portion of the $100 that we were given for expenses aboard the ship.

I am entering a subscription to TIME magazine to be sent to me in Rangoon. I have also purchased a large dictionary, which I have long wanted.

I hope Wayne is growing to be a big boy and that his Mamma, Pappa, Grandmamma, and Uncle James are well and happy.

Now that we are really going, I am kinda' getting the cold feet.

When we really haul anchor and cast free from the wharf and the nose of the ship points its way through the Golden Gate out into the vast Pacific, I know that a mingled feeling of sorrow at leaving the good old USA and joy at anticipating new lands and adventure will sweep over me.

Be good and each help take care of the other until I get back and can help, too.

My best love to all of you,

John, Jr.

5. A SHIP IS SUCH A SMALL AND LARGE THING AT ONCE

Finally, they have set sail on the M.S. Boschfontein, a Dutch passenger ship. In this long letter that is missing the first and last page, John records his thoughts each day.

He explains there are 15 different nationalities on board, and he's fascinated by the vast differences in culture. Friendly and sociable, he meets many people. He learns that missionaries have been working in China since the 1800s, bringing Western religion and education and medical care. Missionaries on board who have worked in China tell him about some of the conditions he will face.

A Chinese man who has just spent a year at Harvard offers to teach John some of his native language.

Still, no one discusses the reason for their trip, and John and his fellow pilots and mechanics have fictitious occupations listed on their passports.

Under a veil of secrecy, the AVG will be onboard this ship for weeks. For safety, the ship's name has been removed, smoking is forbidden on deck at night, and the windows below are covered for a "blacked-out" effect.

News arrives every day through International Morse Code, which was transmitted wirelessly from the transatlantic telegraph cable. The tones and clicks transmitted were translated and printed for the passengers to keep up with world news. (The last telegraph was sent in 2013, although modern technology has long since replaced this form of communication.)

This is the first letter where John hints of danger. Rumors abound of mounting guns on the ship, which John feels will only make them a target. Even though the U.S. is not at war, John was leery of Japan and didn't trust them.

Most amazing in this particular letter is John's foresight. Although he's only 26 years old, he imagines a plan for a "Central International Government," that would bring about "understanding and friendship between different races."

In January 1942, four months after this letter was written—and a month after Pearl Harbor was bombed—the concept of the United Nations is first announced by President Franklin Roosevelt. Soon, 26 nations will come together and pledge to fight the Axis Powers.

En route San Francisco to Honolulu

There are over 200 missionaries in China. There are about 25 on this boat. They are interesting but shy people.

Catholics have more missionaries in China than have the Protestants, because they started earlier. Baptists, Methodists, Presbyterians, etc., have their own areas in which to work. Apparently this cuts down competition. The area that each church will have to work in is allotted by a central committee.

How they can reconcile the religion they preach to the slaughter of human beings that they witness is beyond me. These missionaries tell gruesome tales of bombings, mass killings, and of having to flee for their lives. They have witnessed guerilla warfare by the Chinese, which causes the enemy no end of trouble.

On board the boat we have to be more careful of our language than we may perhaps otherwise be.

Some missionaries only teach religion to the natives. Others, who are more liberal and progressive, teach them how to grow more and better crops; set up schools and hospitals; teach more of a social gospel.

I wish someone would be more social to me. I lost $10 in a poker game last night. Perhaps it was the best thing. It certainly convinced me that I am not a poker player, and I'll not try that again.

The missionaries say that in occupied areas of China, the Chinese who remain wear badges of identification. When guerilla bands come in at night and destroy roads, telegraph lines, blow up buildings, etc., the Chinese who are there are made to repair and rebuild the damage.

The best thing about this boat is the food. It is remarkably good. We dine better than the best restaurants that I have ever been into. It is an amazement to all of us how they serve such perfect food. You can have all that you want of any or all of an average of 50 selections at each meal. Since the menu in part is in Dutch, one gets a pleasant surprise trying new dishes. The Javanese waiters are excellent, but do not speak English, thus each item on the menu is numbered and you point to whatever numbered item you wish.

An average dinner menu will include any or all of 8 different kinds of fruit juices: apple, grape, orange, loganberry, pineapple, grapefruit, etc., any or all of 6 or more different kinds of salad, fixed exquisitely, soups of different kinds, a cold buffet table that makes you want to devour everything on it. In the way of cooked meats you can have delicious baby beef steaks which are very tender, goose, rabbit, grilled ham, veal, chicken livers, etc., together with 5 or 6 different kinds of fish; fruits include apples, oranges, pears, etc., potatoes are prepared any of a dozen different ways, and a choice of half a dozen different vegetables. When you finally get ready for dessert you want to eat every one on the menu but because you are already filled to the brim you have to eat ice cream, cake, pie, or some choice preparation of a fruit cocktail, etc. The Dutch really have the word on pastries. You should see some of the things they fix up—or have I already made you hungry enough?

Maybe I'm just trying to get myself hungry. Mealtime rolls around so fast that I don't have time to develop an appetite, and I want to kick myself in the pants for not being able to eat more when I get to the table.

Another thing that that takes the sharpness away from any appetite that I might be able to develop is that mid-morning they bring around fruit juices and cookies for everybody. Again at 4 in the afternoon they serve tea (and I'm getting to like it) together with more cakes. Then at night about 9:30 they bring around sandwiches, cookies, and more tea!

One of the nicest things is the silver, dishes, and glassware that they have. At each place is four knives, three forks, three spoons, four plates, two glasses, and one cup and a large fresh napkin. At each table are large bowls of fresh cut flowers: carnations, snapdragons, fern, zinnias, roses, etc. The dining room itself is impressive. The ship is a combination freighter-passenger type. Apparently there are very few all passenger ships left. The Army and Navy have taken most of them for troop ships. These days there isn't the passenger volume that there was before the war. Passports are difficult to obtain. We have aboard over one hundred passengers. The capacity is about 150. While there is room for more passengers, there is no space for more cargo. The fore and aft decks and the hole are filled with trucks for Rangoon.

The passenger deck has ample chairs, tables, games, etc. There are also two large lounges and one bar room. Two or three loudspeakers emit modern melodies from an electric player. There is a laundry, beauty and barber shop, library, showers, badminton court, and writing desks.

Each morning at 10 we get wireless bulletins, which are posted and deal mostly with events in the international situation. We learned yesterday that six flyers were killed at Pensacola, but their names were not given.

WATER, WATER, WATER–you wouldn't believe it possible. Where does it all come from?

All day long nothing but water. After a night's sleep, again in the morning all one can see is WATER, WATER, WATER.

Yesterday we had our first Abandon Ship Drill. Life preservers are above the closets in our room. I am in Life Boat #2.

Every night we are blacked-out. All port holes are kept closed if lights are on in the cabin. A tarpaulin is stretched around the deck and windows are closed with blind shutters. No one smokes on deck. Navigation and running lights are out. There are as many lights on in the passenger area of the ship as in normal times, but if you investigate one will see that the ship is completely blacked-out. The ship's captain has orders to run from any ship that is spotted on the horizon. A constant watch is kept by look-outs with powerful glasses. Last night another ship was spotted and the course was changed and full speed employed, but the other ship caught up. It was a Dutch destroyer making 40 knots. The best this ship can do is 17 knots and cruises at about 15. No radios are allowed as an ordinary-looking radio may be a harmful sending set. No one is allowed on the bridge or in the engine rooms. Consequently, though we know that we should be half-way to Hawaii, we may be going around in circles. One indication that we are on our way is that it is getting perceptibly warmer. Our course from San Francisco is West by South. Some members of the ship's crew have already warned us that it will be plenty hot and stuffy aboard when we get to the Tropics and observe black-outs.

The Dutch have long been famous for their ships, which have sailed every ocean and sea. This ship belongs to The Netherlands Navigation Steamship Co. and was one of their fleet of 22 ships. Now, the only four ships that are left of this fleet, due to sinking during the war, operate out of Batavia, Java (in the Dutch East Indies), under the Java Pacific Line.

The Dutch members of the crew, this includes all the ship officers and engineers together with the cooks, have not been home in over two years. Their families are in Holland. They cannot send money home as the company will not allow it because the Germans will confiscate it. As long as Germany occupies The Netherlands these men and ships cannot go home. One of the officers was going to be retired, with a pension, after returning home when they sailed from Amsterdam two years ago on what was scheduled to be a five-week trip to Central America. Three weeks out, Holland was invaded. The ship had to continue on into the Pacific and has been operating in these waters since.

The Dutch language written and spoken is much like German, but you insult them if you say so. Most Dutch are down on Great Britain for not invading Germany, failing to help the countries that she promised military aid to if they were invaded, sending her New Zealand, Australian and Canadian troops to do all the dirty service required by her armies. This much I agree with them. From that point on you can detect a jealous rivalry establishing colonial possessions. The Dutch will point with pride to their East Indies and then ask that you go to Bombay and see the thousands that sleep in the street at night, the dirt and filth, and the lack of proper care of the inhabitants.

There is no question but that the people of The Netherlands believe in and practice cleanliness. The condition of the ship is proof enough for that.

There are two ways of classifying tonnage of ships. Really, there are three ways: water displacement, weight of the ship, and cargo tonnage. This ship has a water displacement of about 14,000 tons; the ship weighs about 5,000 tons and can carry a cargo weight of 7,000 tons.

There is a ship's crew of about 150 composed of about 50 Dutch officers, engineers, and cooks; about 50 Javanese waiters and cabin boys; and 50 Chinese sailors.

Among the passengers there are 7 or 8 Chinese mechanics. They have had a two-month familiarization course in Allison engines at the General Motors Allison factory in Indianapolis. All of them are American citizens and have had a year or two of college training. They are bound for Rangoon. They may be scheduled to work with us on the Burma Road. The planes that we will fly will have Allison engines.

There are several posters about the ship warning that "Careless talk costs lives." Since we have been warned not to repeat anything at all about our mission, there is considerable restraint among the passengers. I dare say that not another one of the fellows in our bunch knows that these Chinese boys mentioned above are going to Rangoon or that they are mechanics and are going to work on P-40's in Rangoon.

All the different groups above stay strictly to their own groups.

I have ventured forth some, however, and found considerable interesting information.

Four other flyers not in our group are bound for the Dutch East Indies and are under contract to teach Dutch students there how to fly. One of the fellows in this group has been a flight instructor in Canada for two years. Another has ferried bombers to England and ferried different military aircraft to various places within England for a period of six months. He tells about bombings he has been in, but particularly I was interested in his criticism of the English for their inefficiency. This was borne out by narratives of another of the group. The English it seems are noted for two or three things: first, the manner in which they "muddle through" everything that they do–and how in the situation today they don't do anything at all; second, that England has always looked after England's interests first, last, and foremost; third, class distinction.

These flyers say that the foremost question on an Englishman's lips is, "When is the United States coming into the war?" One of this group says that some Lord-in-the-bush or sump'n asked him, "What is the USA waiting for–England to win the war?" England did not consider it of sufficient importance to help the Czechs, nor the Poles. And they accomplished a wonderful feat of evacuation at Dunkirk when Holland, Belgium, and France were invaded. Russia now needs their help and is receiving practically none. If Russia loses and England really has to fight to survive, they will, but not without hollering with every breath for the USA to save them.

The further I get away from embarkation the more I hear about what a "fall guy" Uncle Sam is for every hard luck story he hears.

It might be better and much cheaper for the USA to mind her own business at home and arm to the teeth to defend herself. This she cannot do because the world is becoming smaller. She has to enter into relationships with every country and court their favor but not by being a "dupe." Uncle Sam should be more hard-boiled.

There is a sharp, intelligent-looking Chinese aboard who has spent one year at Harvard with a Rockefeller scholarship and won an M.A. degree in Psychology. He has promised to teach me some Chinese.

There are several dialects among Chinese. Those from northern China cannot understand the people from South China though the written language is the same. The official Chinese language is Mandarin. This same fellow that is to teach me Chinese is helping another Chinese learn to speak Mandarin. This latter fellow is from Southern China and speaks Cantonese.

One of the Chinese mechanics born in the US is making his first trip to China. He says he likes this much better than being drafted.

The ship travels a distance of about 375 nautical miles in 24 hours. After a couple days aboard the ship one almost becomes oblivious to the beating of the motors, as they make a deep thud, thud, thud, thud, sounding like a heartbeat. It is a little more difficult to forget the continuous pitch, yaw, and roll of the ship. The sea has been as calm and the days as beautiful as when we left the California coast.

Today is another beautiful sight. Water everywhere covered with gentle whitecaps. The sun is shining brightly, and it is getting much warmer than when we left San Francisco.

This is the 5th day, Sunday, September 28. We should be about 1875 nautical miles from San Francisco. San Francisco is about Lat. 37.5 and Long. 122. We should now be at about Latitude 25 and Long. 147, which means that our course has been approximately South-West. We will probably cross the equator before getting to Rangoon. This will depend upon the course we follow. I understand that we will stay in Java about 5 days.

The Sunday morning services were usual church services

despite the fact that most of those that attended were Missionaries. A young missionary tried to explain how we could be saved despite the fact that all had sinned and the Lord would accept only those who were perfect. This could be accomplished he said because Jesus gave his life in redemption for our sins.

That we will mount guns on the ship at Surabaya is being rumored. Gun turrets are already constructed fore and aft. This will make our situation somewhat more dangerous as most armed merchant ships are sunk without warning. It would give us a better chance should we encounter surface raiders, i.e. provided the accuracy of our gunners is better than that of our opponents'.

Already I am getting a much better idea of the geography of the world. Upon talking to several of the passengers who talked about such places as Calcutta, Sydney, Amsterdam, and Singapore with familiarity that I would use when talking about Selma, Dothan, and Birmingham, I found it necessary to get a better idea of the relative positions of the different countries. I was amazed at my own ignorance in this matter. For example, I have just found out that Surabaya is about 10 degrees below the equator and that Bali, that island of song and romance, is just a short distance south. My new dictionary says that the population of Bali is 950,000. Population of other places: Rangoon, India (the Rangoon I am destined for is in Burma. If there is one in India, I do not know of it) 342,000; Chunking 635,000; China, 474,487,000; Burma, Ind (Prov), I get it now, Burma must be a province of India. India in turn is a territorial possession of England, population 14,667,000; Hong Kong, 978,000; Singapore, 597,000; Batavia, 435,000; Sumatra, 5,867,000; Peiping, 1,300,000; Tsinan, 621,000; Shanghai, 3,490,000. All these figures are larger than I had anticipated.

Some people go to all parts of the world. It amazes me how Americans can find themselves so far from home.

I want no part of being in the Engineering department on a ship. The engineers on this ship stay below, have no deck of their own, and what they do with the few hours that they have off is a puzzle to me. Once in a while one can see one or two of them getting a breath of fresh air on the cargo deck. The Chinese sailors have an after-deck and occasionally they can be seen there. In the bow of the ship is a small deck for steerage passengers. It is surprising to me how the different groups aboard can remain so segregated, considering they have such small quarters. A ship is such a small and large thing at once.

The only possible solution that I can see to ever ensure any permanent peace on earth is for all nations to belong to a League of Nations or some sort of Central International Government. This government will have the only Army or military organization. Individual nations may maintain their own police organization, as do the cities and states of the U.S. The International Army will be used only to enforce laws and prevent wars between nations. When this comes about maybe an International Language can be agreed upon. This will help more than any single thing to bring about understanding and friendship between different races.

On board this boat at least 15 different nationalities are represented, each of which has their own language. Throughout the world are hundreds of different languages. How much closer one common language would bring people together.

If the English should lose the war they would leave their island kingdom and move to Canada. This may come about in another generation, anyway, says an Englishman on the boat.

He tells interesting stories about Nazi trickery, bribery, subterfuge, propaganda, and other efforts to undermine solidarity in England before the war. This Nazi effort has gained great strength. Other countries were similarly weakened and were easily invaded.

6. CROSSING THE EQUATOR

After a stopover in Hawaii, John remarks how similar it was to San Diego—rapid growth, great weather, and a big presence of military personnel. They are now heading to Surabaya, Indonesia's second-largest city and the capital of East Java.

When pulling away from the harbor, they encounter a suspicious Japanese fishing boat. The ship's crew believes the fishermen will inform Tokyo of their ship's movements—because the same thing had happened when they left San Francisco. Following that incident, the AVG group offered to take two-hour turns standing watch in the crow's nest.

The 400-year-old tradition of celebrating the crossing of the equator is that of a mariner "slimy pollywog" transitioning into a "trusty shellback." Officially called "Neptune's Court," it included outlandish dress, crowns, slipping and sliding, and imbibing—a ritual everyone participated in. After being smeared with fish parts, each person was dumped from a chair into a make-shift pool—injuries were the norm.

This commemoration was practiced on other passenger ships like the Klipfontein, Jagerfontein, Bloemfontein, and the President Pierce, which had transported the other AVG personnel heading to Rangoon.

John writes about meeting a survivor of the HMS Brittania and hearing his story of courage and survival. The Brittania sank after being torpedoed by a German UB-50 sub in 1918, just two days before the Armistice ending the First World War was signed on November 11, 1918.

Three days before reaching Surabaya, the passengers are instructed to surrender their cameras. John believes this is censorship "run into the ground," and he is certain any pictures they might have were already taken by "Japs" and the Germans.

John warns of censorship in his future letters because they are traveling to parts of the world that are at war. He isn't certain what will be allowed and what is likely to be censored.

En route Honolulu to Surabaya

Everyone hated to leave Hawaii. Honolulu is a boomtown similar to San Diego. We know that three weeks will pass before we set foot on land again.

There are many Philippines, Chinese, Japanese, and mixed nationalities there. The price of automobiles is sky-high. It is almost impossible to find living quarters despite new homes being built everywhere. Rent, food, and all living expenses are way up but so are wages. Some of the people there fear what is going to happen when the boom explodes. Hawaii is pretty but not more scenic than many places I've seen in California. I had just as soon swim in Santa Monica as Waikiki Beach. The entire place is principally Army and Navy.

As we pulled out of the harbor about 8 p.m., a Japanese fishing boat came alongside, and it was quite obvious that two of her crew were trying to find the name of our ship. Our ship carries no name or flag and is painted war gray. The Chief Engineer said that the same thing happened when we left San Francisco. The ship's officers believe that these Japanese fishing boats are operated by Japs who have been trained in Naval Service at home and have wireless equipment on board. This is very likely true. There are thousands of

Japanese fishermen who haunt every port on the West coast. They could easily inform Tokyo of the movements of every ship, including American man-of-war, since they haunt San Pedro Harbor in countless numbers.

The second day out our gang offered to stand look-out in the crow's nest. Each of us stands this watch at two-hour stretches throughout the day. The perch is about 100 feet above the main deck and the visibility is about 18 miles in all directions under normal conditions. A phone connects directly with the Bridge. So far we have not spotted another ship. I understand that most raiders have airplanes, which they launch to make observations. The plane can determine the course of any ship that it spots, and the raider can set out in pursuit. To affect this, our ship changes course every so often. If we should spot another ship, we would immediately attempt to run out of sight.

It was surprising how warm the water was when we were along the equator. Water taken directly from the sea was actually hot. After pouring it into the swimming pool it cooled somewhat. We are now 700 or more miles from the equator. A testimonial to the fact that I have crossed the equator is a shaved head. This is a result of joining the "Order of the Neptune." You should see our boys looking like a bunch of Germans with hair about ½ inch long. They will long remember crossing the equator.

Deck tennis is one of the favorite games. I spend at least three hours per day acquiring muscles and a tan. I have not had more of either since 1933. As a result I feel excellent! Except for restlessness, which all of us have a bad case of. Life aboard a ship confines one's activities to a very small area.

From now on every letter that I mail and receive will be censored. What the censor will and won't allow, I don't know as yet. This censoring business holds up the mail, and I hear that it takes two or three months to get a letter to or from the U.S. An Englishman aboard says that when he arrived in Bermuda from Lisbon, he discovered there were 14,000 stacks of mail waiting to be censored. This despite the fact there were two or 300 censors working 24 hours per day, seven days per week. They read every letter completely, and if any part of it is ambiguous or not written in clear English, it is cut or stamped out. One may get a letter "Dear so and so" with a few ands, thes, and buts with everything else stamped out. The censorship will probably be rigid in Rangoon. Also air mail rates from Rangoon to the States is $1.20 American money per half ounce. Speaking of money, I have found that one cannot send money out of any of these countries to the U.S. without permission, which is practically impossible to get. If gifts are sent the recipient has to pay duties in the U.S., which often amounts to more than the item is worth. Consequently it seems that this answers the problem about Xmas presents. I will wait and bring some things back with me when I return, as they will be allowed duty free under a classification of household goods.

Today is the third day aboard ship. The day is beautiful—ideal. The sunsets and moon rises have been the most beautiful I have ever seen. The Southern Cross is distinctly visible every night. We are now a hop-skip-and-a-jump from the Australian shore. We will pick up a pilot there tomorrow to take us through the Straits, which, I understand, in addition to being narrow are also mined. Ever since Hawaii we have seen flying fish. It is a marvel to me how they float through the air without moving their wings at all. They don't move with the slow grace of a seagull, but dart along at terrific speeds, dive into the water, then twenty feet farther emerge again and continue their gliding.

Some of the names from the passenger list: Fong Fook Yew, Fu Hong Wu, Lum Son Git, Pak On Lee, Tau Hau. Recent books that I have read: Burma Road, Through China's Wall or Through The China Wall, Berlin Diary, September issue of Fortune, which is overrun with information about China, technical manuals on Air Navigation, Yang and Yin, etc.

Did I tell you about the Egyptian passenger on board who survived 23 days in a life-boat in the Atlantic after the ship Britannia, which he was on, was sunk by a German man-of-war? The Britannia was a large 40,000 tonner out of Liverpool bound for Cape Town. They spotted the man-of-war and after recognizing the Britannia they hoisted the English flag, when the naval ship came closer they took down the English flag and raised the German swastika and then opened fire. The Britannia, being armed with 5- or 6-inch guns, fought back for 40 or 50 minutes then gave up. When the passengers were in the life boats the Germans put a torpedo in her. The Egyptian was one of 87 in one boat. The heat of the day and the cold of the night killed off many of them. They ran out of food but because of good fortune of rain it was managed to keep a bare supply of drinking water. They saw several ships and sent up rockets but the ships would turn away. Incidentally, the reason the ships do this is because sometimes submarines set out little life rafts and when some unsuspecting ships come along to rescue, alas they are sunk. Forty-four of the 87 died before they managed to get to land, which was on the coast of Brazil. It is a pathetic story of how each day one or two would die and be tossed overboard. Every day the officer-in-charge promised that they would make land in another couple days. Some went crazy and jumped overboard. When they finally reached land, they were so weak they could hardly climb out of the boat. Fortunately, they were found by a fisherman, and all had to be hospitalized.

Our celebration of crossing the equator was probably the roughest toughest battle of the century. It had been planned for days. Neptune's court was all rigged up in outlandish dress. Cut-up smelly fish was put into the mouths of every passenger initiate along with a gooey paste, which was spread on with a floor mop. Since nobody offered themselves voluntarily, they had to be chased and pulled, dragged, and carried to the throne of Neptune. Lastly the initiate was seated in a chair and tipped in the pool. Everyone has minor scratches and bruises. What a rough-and-tumble good time!

From Honolulu we came southwest to Santa Cruz Island and thence West to Cairns, Australia, whence we sailed the sea coast northward staying within the Great Barrier Reef of the Coral Sea until Cape York and thence we departed through the Torres Straight (between New Guinea and Australia). We are now in the Flores Sea, a couple of days from Surabaya. From there we will go to Batavia and thence to Singapore and then through the Strait of Malacca past the Malay States to Siam and then to Burma. After talking to the barber, it seems we came a more Southerly course from Hawaii to below the Samoa Islands and then to Cairns.

Yesterday they had everyone turn in their cameras. Their reason was that they did not want any pictures of the Islands taken. We are now three days out from Surabaya. Sometimes, I think, officious censorship restriction on taking pictures can be run into the ground. If all the pictures we could take collectively were handed over to the Japs or Germans, they would probably be torn up as these are two Nations that already have accurate maps and better pictures which they have collected for years.

Have just finished reading "Keys of the Kingdom" by Cronin. This is probably not his best book. It smacks of Yang and Yin. There is a classical Chinese on the ship who has with him his wife—a white woman—she looks the role she plays. A happy-go-lucky friendly missionary with his wife going to India. He has served 25 years in Japan and Korea and was run out last year. They never give up. The missionaries have turned out to be real friendly people. None of them drink, cuss, or smoke—but spend their time in conversation, reading, writing, and playing deck games. I have enjoyed several long chats with a small pleasant fellow who works for U.S. Rubber Co. in Sumatra and has for 13 years. The Javanese and Chinese workers on the rubber plantations make an average 20¢ per day for 10 hours work. When they don't work they don't get paid.

For the past several days the sea has been as calm as glass and as beautiful as a flower. The weather is getting warmer as we approach the equator again. Whenever we come within sight of land, the news spreads around the ship, and everyone is leaning over the rail on the top deck looking very wistful. Though the water is a delightful blue-green color, you begin to wonder if there is no end to it, after looking at it for days and days without seeing land.

Initiation into Order of Neptune

Crossing the Equator October 12, 1941
(Captions by John Donovan)
National Naval Aviation Museum collection

National Naval Aviation Museum collection. John Donovan aboard the M.S. Boschfontein, holding a copy of Burma Road by Nicol Smith. This book, published in 1940, was highlighted in a Saturday Evening Post article, which described the book as a travelogue. The columnist, "Quivis," wrote: "If entertainment is what the reader is in search of, they will get what they are looking for."

7. NO WORKEE–NO PAYEE

A month after leaving San Francisco, John is watching workers unload cargo in Semarang, Java. His letters read like a social commentary as he tells his family about the low wages, the harm the white-man cigarettes have caused, and how the women wash laundry in the filthy water that runs through the city's gutters.

John's observations about the locals are details some might not notice. He compares their lives to those in the rest of the world—always seeing more than what meets the eye.

He and his recruit group encounter six AVG members on their way back to the United States following their unpleasant experience in Rangoon. Dysentery, poor accommodations, and terrible food were their major complaints. John and his fellow recruits are not swayed and decide to form their own opinion about Rangoon after they've experienced it themselves.

Oct. 24, 1941

In The Netherlands East Indies

It is now one month since we departed San Francisco. We are in an entirely different part of the world altogether.

I have been overcome with some of the different sights that I have seen. At this moment we are at anchor in the harbor of Semarang, Java. It is 9 p.m. The Javanese workers are as yet unloading cargo. They have been busy at this task since early morning. Most of the passengers are sitting around the deck talking in groups; several are writing; some are reading; others are leaning over the rail watching the unloading going on. It is surprising the amount and variety of cargo that a ship this size carries. Some of the fellows took a trip to Bali from Surabaya, a distance of about 250 miles. They tell some interesting stories about cock fights, monkey dances, a beautiful beach, and wonderful wood-carving objects being so very cheap.

It has amazed me, the infinite patience and skill which it must take to carve into hard wood the symbols and pictures that one finds on all kinds of furniture. These woodcarving objects can be bought so cheap that it is pitiful. An American dollar is worth $1.80 in Dutch money. One hundred cents in Dutch money makes one guilder. They do not use the word dollar, but they do use the word cents and their coins are in the same denominations as ours. If you were speaking of $1.80, one would say "one guilder and eighty cents." All this brings up the subject of the cheapness of native labor here in the Indies.

There are many rice, coffee, and rubber plantations on the island of Java that pay their men laborers 8¢ and the women workers 5¢ per day in Dutch money, or about half the amount in American money. This means twelve-hour days and seven days per week. No workee–no payee. On the street of Surabaya they have a couple of large steam rollers. Standing in front or sitting behind the large wheel as it rolls over hot asphalt is a worker who keeps the wheel moist by wetting it continually with a brush and cleaning it with a scraper. For a full-day's work he gets paid 10 Dutch cents per day. I have visited in several American and Dutch homes here, and the custom is to pay their servants 14 or 15 guilders per month. This would be $7 or $8 American dollars per month. Those servants come at 6 o'clock in the morning and are off work when the family is through with them, sometimes 2 or 3 o'clock the next morning. Labor here is cheaper than machinery. Whereas a gallon of gasoline costs 45 American cents, one could hire all the labor he wanted at half that amount per day. The Dutch are anxious to continue this wage scale and anxiously discourage Americans from paying the natives too much for services rendered. Whereas they endeavor in every way "to keep the native in his place" they themselves are out for all they can get. One of their restaurants that I stopped in last night charged 60¢ for a Coca-Cola and 50¢ for a very plain ham sandwich–Dutch money. They charge those prices for food but are boastful that the natives can live on 2¢ worth of food per day. After traveling around Semarang today and seeing the natives eat, I can believe this. Many of them ate out of leaves a substance that is supposed to be rice with a substance that is supposed to be chopped meat spread over it. If that wouldn't make you sick, seeing them washing clothes certainly would. Along the streets run a gutter as in any good city. Through this gutter in Semarang runs a certain amount of very filthy water. Today must have been wash day. Several hundred native women were standing in these gutters washing their clothes. Whenever they wished to relieve themselves, they just squatted down and proceeded without any compunction or hesitation. The surprising thing was that the clothes had a certain resemblance to being clean after the so-called washing.

I don't think that I will ever smoke another cigarette in my life. The white man has brought his cigarette to the Indies and managed to get all of them in the habit of smoking them. Consequently the native toils long hours for a few pennies a day and then takes half his earnings and buys cigarettes. He smokes these assiduously. For those who only make 10¢ per day there are native cigarettes for 3, 4, 5 cents per package. Coming back to the boat at night and seeing the native longshoreman sleeping on the ground on the edge of the street, with an occasional one awake smoking a cigarette is a disheartening sight. The longshoremen here make 20 to 70 cents per day, Dutch money, and most of them sleep out on the streets at night. Offhand, I would say that three-fourths of the natives sleep on the ground. The white people here do not have nearly the conveniences or recreational facilities that we have in the U.S., but their standard of living is so far above that of the natives that a comparison of an about $15 per week clerk to an American millionaire would not be nearly as vast a difference.

When a native gets tired he squats. This position would cramp me considerable and be highly uncomfortable. Personally, if I was that close to the ground I would just sit down. Instead, they sit on their heels and calves with the bottom of their feet on the ground, smoke a cigarette, and seem mighty restful. The Javanese are slight of stature, and I have yet to see one fat Javanese. They are peaceful people, and their Mohammed or Muslim faith makes fatalists of them. They figure what is to be, is to be.

It is now 11 p.m., and the native workers have finished their task and departed. I watched them closely as they filed past, getting into their boat that would take them back to shore. Many were boys about 15, others men about 40. They were a dirty, smelly, tattered lot. I think of what they have to go home to. Then I think of the world over. These natives do not have imagination, ingenuity, and ambition.

People in all parts of the world fit into this category. That is what makes a certain portion of the population in the U.S. performing the most menial tasks and others dependent on society for their support. The natives here are used by the Dutch for their labor value, and the Dutch do not attempt to educate them except for whatever purposes they can better serve the Dutch. In the U.S. we give our Negroes a much better break. The Dutch are proud that the natives are so easily managed. It is true that the natives are very peaceful, they do not drink alcohol in any form, which is a great help in maintaining order. The natives run their own government, police, fire, street repair, etc. Yet, the white man is here to make money, and he makes thousands for every cent the natives make. The only reason that 99% of the white people here have come to the Indies is because they can make more money here than in their home country. Their hope is to someday go back to their native land and retire.

Never before have the circumstances of my birth been considered so fortunate by me. The fact that I happened to be born of white parents and born in America is a source of envy to many in this part of the world. In many shops and stores that I have visited, I have seen many intelligent-looking natives express a soulful wish that they lived in America. Natives here who have some white blood in them are very proud of the fact and consider themselves very much above the others—and indeed, they prosper much more. Those who have a mixture of Chinese or Japanese also seem to do better.

I certainly committed a faux pas the other day. I was in a bookstore and a very attractive girl was waiting on me. She could speak eight languages. It seemed to me that she was a little darker than a full-blooded white person should be. She had been very nice, and I thought I would ask her about it quite frankly. I asked her what nationality she was. With a voice that felt like a ton of ice had hit me, she said, “I am Dutch.” I don’t think that I will ask anyone else that question. Of course she was Dutch—all citizens, natives included, of the Dutch East Indies are Dutch! But she certainly was not going to tell me whether or not she was part colored.

Americans are a funny lot. Gifted because of accident of birth to a land that is the envy of the whole world—particularly now since the rest of the world is in chaos—they are richer than any other people. They are noted for the fact that they won’t speak any other language except English. People born in other parts of the world cannot get away with learning just one language. Most of the countries on the continent of Europe are no larger than one of the States in the U.S. Therefore, if you were born in Holland, for example, in grade school and high school you learn Dutch, English, French, and German. If you planned on traveling, one would learn, in addition, Spanish, Malay, or Italian, Russian, or any of a dozen other languages. We Americans learn English (?) (I have talked to people who can speak better English than I—and in addition can speak a half dozen other languages) and expect the rest of the world to learn English, too—so they can understand us.

Personally, I am glad that English is the most universal of all languages, because at learning a foreign language, I am a dud. I managed to get a year’s credit in Spanish. After trying for a year and a half, I managed to get no credit in Latin. I tried French and gave up in disgust. If ever I learn a foreign language, it will be because I learned it orally and not from a book.

The last two days the Javanese celebrated their New Year. The most noticeable evidence of their celebration was the explosion of fireworks everywhere. Then, too, they were dressed in brighter clothes and seemed a bit cleaner. It is odd to see a Javanese dressed in a shirt, tie, American coat with a sarong, and no shoes. Sometimes they wear a complete American white linen suit, but no shoes. Sometimes they can be seen dressed in pajamas. The coolie workers wear sarongs, shorts of every description—some of them look like underwear—and undershirts or any kind of shirt or no shirt at all. The Hindus wear a black fez cap, and the Moslems wear a wrap-around turban that looks like a bandana, except that they are more subdued in color. The women wear blouses like American women and sarongs. Some wear American clothes complete. Less than 10% of the natives wear shoes of any kind. Some wear light open sandals. The sarongs that the men and women wear are not the kind Dotty Lamour wears. These here are wrapped around their waists and extend almost to the ground, resembling a long skirt more than anything else. In Semarang I noticed that most of the native women in the large market place were chewing tobacco or snuff, I couldn't tell which—but whatever it was, it didn't look very tempting.

We are getting an excellent chance to see the islands here. In all we will be here about two weeks. We spent 3 days in Surabaya, one day in Semarang, and we are now on our way to Batavia where we will stay for 4 days. Then we go back to Surabaya for 3 more days. All this going up and down the coast is to discharge cargo. It will be about the 10th of November before we get to Rangoon. Most of us plan on taking the train back to Surabaya from Batavia. By doing this we will go through Bandung, which is in the mountains and supposedly a nice cool city. Anyway, we will get to see the island of Java from one end to the other, which means that we will see the agriculture area.

They cannot grow oranges, grapefruit, pears, etc. One orange costs 15¢. They do grow small size bananas, which are very cheap. A pound of grapes that in the U.S. would sell for 10¢ costs 50¢ to $1. Radios, refrigerators, automobiles, etc., are very, very expensive. There is a 33% duty on most imports. A thousand dollar American car costs two thousand American dollars here–refrigerators, radios, the same. There is a great deal of Western influence. On a principal street one can see Buick, Chevrolet, Ford dealers as well as Max Factor stores–signs advertising Arrow shirts, Singer sewing machines, Pebeco toothpaste, etc. However, the main street is dissimilar to the main street of an American city in many more ways. Small Fiat, Austin, and Ford taxis together with horse-drawn carriages furnish public transportation. In Surabaya, streetcars and busses are always crowded with natives. In Semarang where there are fewer white people, bicycles of the tricycle type with a seat in front, horse-drawn carriages, and an occasional auto taxi are the only means of public transportation. You have never seen so many bicycles in all your life. I would estimate that in Surabaya there are 50,000 bicycles.

American films are the only kind shown in theatres. I went to see "The Great Lie," which I did not see in the States. The film is the same except that at the bottom Dutch captions are flashed on as an actor speaks. If you understand English the film can be enjoyed just as if seen in an American theatre.

American songs are heard frequently. Whenever a bunch of Americans get together they always break out in singing "Roll Out the Barrel," "Notre Dame Fight Song," or some other college song, or a folk song like "Old Black Joe." If an American travels to a foreign country, I would first advise him to learn all the old popular songs–and especially the words. Though I cannot carry a tune, I seem to remember the words pretty well as a result of singing them at camps for so long.

In Surabaya we met six fellows who had stayed six weeks in Rangoon and were on their way back to the U.S. They said that it was a little too rough for them. They said that half of the fellows had dysentery, that the city itself was terrible with nothing to do, the food bad, they slept in barracks, and despite the fact that CAMCO tried their best, that they wouldn't stay there for twice the money and were only too glad to have been let out of their contracts and be on their way back home. This was not particularly encouraging for us, but we agreed that they were the kind of fellows who shouldn't have come over in the first place. After we have been in Rangoon ourselves awhile, we will better qualify to voice an opinion. Those six that left constituted 10% of those there—who have the kind of jobs we have.

I read in the news posted on the ship that Russia is still holding out, that the new Japanese cabinet has done nothing as yet—that the U.S. is going to train some Chinese pilots and mechanics in the U.S., and that Stimson said that the Army should have a larger air force than presently planned for. The news in general seems to be about the same as when we left the U.S.

We are now in the harbor of Batavia. This is the hottest place we have hit yet. Batavia, as is Surabaya, is located on very flat land with no hills or mountains visible anywhere. The harbor here is very open, shaped like a horseshoe with a shoreline of about 35 miles visible. There are numerous small islands from 2 to 10 miles from the shoreline.

In Surabaya, three of us took a cab one day and went about 50 kilometers (about 30 miles) to a mountain resort called Tretis. It was a most beautiful place. The homes there were the brightest I have ever seen, in color. There were several large swimming pools with high diving platforms and spring boards, as well as slide chutes. It was much cooler there.

We rented small horses, ponies, and rode all over the place. We had a good time.

I have wondered about the public health facilities afforded the natives. Some of the residents of Surabaya said that they have a public hospital there. When I go back, that is going to be one of the "must" things to see. I have seen a woman deliver a baby right on the public street. They take an event of this kind as we would a minor incident. Not even 1% of the births are attended by doctors, I would say. I am speaking of the natives. They give birth to babies in the shade of a tree, where they are working, etc. In parts of the island, the husband goes to bed after the child is born and receives the solicitude and congratulations, and the poor woman goes into the field and works.

8. DUTCH PECULIARITIES

This letter tells a great story about "borrowing" an apartment from Bob Heising, who was an American civilian pilot the group met on the Boschfontein. Apparently, he was not fooled by the fabricated reason the recruits gave for their trip. In fact, in the Flying Tigers memoir "Baa Baa Black Sheep" by Greg "Pappy" Boyington, Heising was quoted as saying, "When I see an Army Air Corps officer with Lafayette Escadrille wings on the bottom of his jacket, and practically kissing you all good-bye at San Francisco, you can't tell me you are a bunch of clergy."

Despite Heising's suspicions, the recruits laughed it off, never revealing the truth.

Did I tell you about the trip that four of us made through Java? We left the boat at Batavia and went by train to Bandung. Never had I imagined that so much rice was grown in the entire world. Before we left the plains, the rice fields were laid out in perfect squares as far as the eye could see. The government owns and operates the irrigation system, which is a marvel. Because of limited water supply in the dry season, different areas are in various stages of planting. While the rice is growing the field is kept covered in about 6 inches of water. The crudest methods are employed. The seeds are sown thick, in a small area and when the plants are about 8 or 10 inches high, they are pulled up by hand and transplanted into the other fields, by hand, with larger spaces between the plants. All this is done with the natives walking in the field knee-deep in mud. Because snakes eat the rats, which eat the rice, the natives let the snakes live. Plowing is done with crude wooden plowshares pulled by water buffalo or oxen. Along the mountain banks the farmers had a harder time of it. But you should see how they avail themselves of every inch of ground. A mountainside will be terraced all the way to the bottom. This means that in the opening or rivulet between each square plot of ground, the water continually trickles downward, feeding each plot of rice land. One would think that one heavy rain would wash the whole thing away, but it doesn't. The natives sell this and eat cheaper rice.

As we got higher into the mountains we first saw rubber plantations and then coffee and tea. The railroad was a narrow gauge affair, but the coaches were air-conditioned. At one stop we took on another locomotive to help the first, as the grades were steeper. We went through one very long tunnel and across many bridges, which seemed awfully flimsy. None of the bridges had any protection on the sides, and the ravines below the bridges were as much as 400 feet deep. I had much rather been in an airplane.

The best thing we could say for Bandung was that it was nice and quiet and cool. Since there was little to do, we slept a great deal. We stayed in the apartment of Heising and Phillips, two fellows who were on the Boschfontein and came to Java to work for KNILM airways. Our staying at their place was rather amusing. We first went to the hotel where the cost was 10 guilders ($5) per day European plan. We decided to go out and see if Heising and Phillips had room for us. When we arrived they were not at home—so we made ourselves at home. Later we found that they were expected back in a couple of days. We told the manager of Alcot Park, as the place was called, that we were friends of Heising and Phillips and that it would be ok for us to stay there—as it was. The apartment was well laid out and new. The porch was equipped with chairs, swing, table, table lamp, etc. The living room was as modern as any American room could be with a very good Philco radio, etc. The dining room had some of the best glassware and dishes I have ever seen. The bed was one of those huge Dutch affairs with Dutch pillows and "Dutch mammas." The bath was one of those Dutch peculiarities, which has a large tile tank full of water with a container so that you can dip into the water with the bucket and pour the water over your head. This, despite the fact that there was a shower with hot and cold water. Dutch toilets, even in the best houses, as this was—are even more confusing. The toilet has no toilet seat and beside the toilet are bottles filled with water. The more American types have toilet paper. I was glad to see this had the American touch. The most amusing thing of all was what we discovered the next morning.

As there seemed to be only one bed we matched and Bob and I won. We slept well. The other two had lost, and one slept on the couch and the other on the lounge in the living room. Neither slept at all that night they said. The next morning we discovered two more bedrooms which contained three more beds. Boy, were they mad. Since it was cool, right after breakfast they went to sleep. In all, we stayed there three days and two nights. We went swimming, went to an active volcano, took pictures, went to the Army airport, and rode in the funny taxis—in this part of the world the taxis are about the funniest thing possible. They have no meters as have American cabs. When you have arrived at your destination, you give the driver whatever you think is right. Sometimes the driver believes he is due more. Particularly this is true of the "rich Americans." We usually end up by giving them more–usually by twice–what the other people here pay, but we have lots of fun arguing. They can't understand English so we see who can make the most nonsensical statements. We will say in a loud angry voice, "So–you think rotten bananas are better than sour pickles, eh! Well, I'll bet you a dollar that a horse can run farther than your bicycle!" We carry on like that until we get tired and then pay him some more. The natives like to bargain. They can spot an American a mile away. They think all of them are rich. We are, compared to their standards. An American standard of living costs more almost anywhere here in the East than it would in the U.S. By now we have become somewhat adept at bargaining. Whatever the natives ask you can usually figure that the correct price is about half that.

9. EXPOSTULATING

Nearing their war-zone destination, John writes what he would do if he were in charge and about the many tragedies war brings. He is sure "Japan is going to do something soon."

This letter was written a month prior to Japan's brutal attack on Pearl Harbor. John won't live to see the end of the war, but it will end because "hell broke loose over Japan"—just as John predicted in this letter.

The group meets Cecil Brown, a correspondent for CBS and author of "Suez to Singapore." Brown worked for CBS from 1940-1943. He resigned after a scolding for reporting, "A good deal of enthusiasm for this war is evaporating into thin air." His reason for resigning was his inability to follow their policy of "non-opinionated reporting." He later went on to work for NBC and ABC. After retiring from broadcasting, he went into teaching.

John Young, NBC correspondent for the Far East, boards the ship in Singapore to get closer to the "show" on the Burma Road. In "Black Sheep One," a biography about Gregory "Pappy" Boyington written by Bruce Gamble, the author writes about the group drinking on board with Young their last night before arriving in Rangoon. Young tells the group how he believes "the Japanese were good fliers and should not be underestimated" but didn't believe Japan was "going to give the U.S. much trouble."

Again, there is no end to the letter—perhaps this time it was due to the champagne celebration at the end of their long voyage.

Nov. 10, 1941

En route Singapore to Rangoon at last! We are on the last leg of our trip. We have been 7 weeks en route. None of us would trade a thousand dollars for our experiences on this trip. We should be in Rangoon in another two days.

There are some miscellaneous ideas I feel like expostulating. The first is that Japan, of course, is going to do something and soon.

When a nation builds a formidable war machine it almost always has to use it. Japan is in a situation where she almost has to do something. The country is terribly overcrowded and has serious economic conditions at home because of being cut off from normal trade relations with other countries. Also, she has already pledged herself to an aggressive policy. I have developed some ideas about countries like Germany, Italy, Japan, and Russia that have followed aggressive policies.

If I were a dictator of the U.S. after this war, I would pledge this country to an active part in maintaining peace throughout the world. As I see it, this can only be accomplished through a League or Federation or Assembly of Nations. All nations would be demilitarized except for a police force within each country. The League would maintain a standing Army and Navy, which would maintain order among the nations. At the first indication of an act of aggression by one nation upon another, the League would dispatch its Army, Navy and Air Force.

The great tragedy in the past has been that other nations sit by and wait until it is too late while a nation like Germany arms itself to the teeth. After reading Berlin Diary, one is impressed with how other nations can be so blind while

Germany prepares to take them into camp. The greatest virtue and tragedy of a democracy are its democratic principles. While I hold to a sociological, humanitarian view toward other nations, I will always temper this with a cold-blooded practical viewpoint. For example, right now if I were president of the U.S. I would send a sufficient amount of the Navy, Army, Marines, and Air Force to the gates of Tokyo. Then I would have a delegation call upon the Japanese officials. If they did not prove sufficiently agreeable to maintain the peace in the Pacific, then I would have the delegation remove itself back to the battleship and then let hell break loose over Japan. This is cruel. However, it is a simpler and more humane way of settling the problem. As it stands now, Japan is causing a case of jitters among all the other countries here in the East. The strain is terrific. It also causes disruption in the normal manner of living of millions of people.

War is a horrible idiocy of human beings. People who cause a war should be dealt with severely. Because there will always be people who will cause wars, the United States, because it is the strongest nation, should not be too concerned in the future about following a strong armed plan for maintaining peace. The lesson that the U.S. should learn from the world disorder at present is that she should not be reluctant to build herself a world empire. Indeed, the western hemisphere should be solidly American—or United States. Should Australia or the East Indies or Timbuktu or any country choose to come within the American sphere, we should not restrain from admitting them simply because of our decadent opposition to empire building.

The nicest, the ideal, is to think that people respect each other's rights. The people engaged in warring upon one another today disprove this. Japan, for example, has waged a war for four years and has killed thousands. No other nation has stepped in to hinder her, although it is to the interests of several nations to do so. By not doing so now, they only delay the fateful day when they will have to defend themselves.

Maintaining the peace should be just as aggressive as maintaining a war.

Have been reading some detective stories and can see that the same thing applies in the prevention of crime. One of the fellows said that the cost of crime in the U.S. exceeds a billion dollars yearly. If we followed an aggressive policy of preventing crime and spent half this amount we would save half a billion yearly and an awful lot of trouble. Instead, we are awful lenient with criminals. Here again, the nicest thing is to think that citizens won't commit crimes. The many crimes committed disprove this. Therefore, we should deal harshly with criminals. We should follow an aggressive policy of preventing crimes.

This business of being brutal with people and nations who plan on being brutal to others is a lazy man's idea of the most expedient, practical, and simplest policy. I approve it. It gives more opportunity to those who have no criminal inclinations to enjoy themselves and affords more opportunity for advancement in science and society. This plan prevents a nation from spending a generation recuperating from the effects of a war only to be thrown into another one.

War brings many tragedies of equal concern as loss of life. Separation from family and loved ones. Many Australians are living in the interior of Malaya, which is definitely not a place for white men. Separation from normal occupations. Breakdown of morality. Engendering of hate. Loss of faith in human nature and purpose of life. People who cause all this should have to pay.

In Singapore we met 7 of the CAMCO boys who had come down

in the Lockheed for a few days from Rangoon to discuss some affairs with the RAF there. Our fellows say that the RAF is about the most uncooperative people possible.

Last night I had an encounter, which sort of convinced me about my aggressive peace policy. I was sitting at a table with four other fellows. We were discussing one of the Chinese on board. One of the fellows—rather stupid and slow-witted—was not following the conversation. He countered with some statement that had nothing to do with the subject under discussion. All of us laughed at him. He singled me out to make an issue of it. Before anyone knew what was happening—especially me—he had gotten up and swung four or five times at me, knocking me on the floor. When I got up to let him have a dose of the same medicine, he was apologizing for what he had done. I forgot my aggressive peace policy and made up with him. Inasmuch as he had attacked me while I was seated, and without warning, I should have made him pay—even as he was offering his hand and apologizing. He said he had been drinking. Later in the night—apparently after more drinking, he caused quite a disturbance and no little embarrassment. I believe that if I had knocked him for a couple of loops he would have calmed down. As he is smaller than I, it will be a relatively simple matter to take care of him at the first provocation. He needs it, as he is the kind of fellow to cause more trouble. Being confined to such close quarters has caused several other fights. The fellows see so much of each other—this with the pent-up emotions that most of us have as a result of being on a ship so long with nothing to do—I attribute as the cause of the other fights. All of us will be glad to get to Rangoon.

Boarding the ship at Singapore for Rangoon was John Young. He has been with NBC for about 12 years. I think that he is going along to see the show on the Burma Road, although he says that he doesn't know whether he will go on to Chungking or over to Calcutta. He, like most Americans here, has his grievances against the British. He wanted to make a broadcast back to the States at Thanksgiving so that we fellows could talk to our folks, but the British censor says that is out because it will give away military positions. Poppycock. Most of us believe that the Japs already know more about what's going on and where than we do. In Singapore, the authorities wouldn't let us take our cameras ashore even though one can rent or buy all the cameras one would want and can have pictures developed everywhere in 24 hours. If the British have anything around that is of any military importance, we didn't see it. They have a few pillboxes mounted on the harbor entrance, a few squadrons of aircraft, and a lot of Australian soldiers. They knew that we were U.S. Navy fliers, yet, they were probably more unfriendly than the Japs. If the U.S. should go to war with Germany and defeat her, the British would claim credit for the victory. Not only that, but she would probably squelch on the billions of dollars-worth of supplies that we have or are sending her. If some British censor cuts any of the above out, it will certainly prove they are more stupid than I had thought.

I am quite convinced that both the Dutch and British have been quite taken aback at the carefree manner in which we have conducted ourselves. For them I can say that some are pretty good fellows, but the majority are stuff shirts who are more interested in making all they can from the cheap native labor. Talking about cheap labor - have you ever seen an entire city block of coal being moved by men carrying a basket load at a time? OR a boat being pushed up a canal by men with long poles (this being cheaper than having a motor in the boat)? Or thousands of rickshaws pulled by men and boys because it is cheaper than riding in a taxi?

Singapore is a busy port with a steady stream of ships moving in and out. The cost of living here is very high. All of us noticed how everything sold is manufactured in the British Empire. Ford cars sold here are made in Canada, likewise Libby's mustard, Heinz's tomato catsup. Kodak films are made in England. The British buy British, and their first and last consideration is for the British. England has made billions from Burma, Malaya, Australia, and India—yet they are hoping the U.S. will keep Japan from taking any of her possessions.

For entertainment during the three days in Singapore we visited the New World, the Great World, and the Happy World. They are all permanent carnivals where they also have large dance halls with Chinese taxi dance girls. We visited the magnificent home and gardens of the Tiger Balm king, a Chinese who has made millions from a home remedy called Tiger Balm, which is supposed to cure anything from the itch to mother-in-law trouble. Most of his gardens are artificial trees and flowers, but it is very difficult to tell the artificial ones from the real thing. He has spent four million dollars on the gardens, which are really gaudy and bare compared to something really beautiful like the Bellingrath Gardens in Mobile, Alabama. The two should not really be compared because they are entirely different. The Tiger Balm affair is mostly temples and concrete walks with lots of paint, bricks, and stone, make believe dragons, etc.

We also met Cecil Brown, who is with CBS and also does a column for Newsweek, I believe. He spent three years in Italy before coming here last April. The main thing about him is that he is very desirous of getting back to the U.S., where he has not been for four years, and seeing his wife again. He has not seen her for a year. He is completely faithful to her, not being willing to have anything to do with a woman here. My bet is that she is completely unfaithful to him.

I forgot to say that along with the apartment in Bondung went meals and servants. The meals were excellent. They were cooked in a general kitchen for all the apartments in the court. You could order practically anything, and all of it was delicious. I hereby declare that the Dutch are tops in preparing food, both as to method and quantity. The houseboy served meals and fetched anything while the maid cleaned up–what the other boy did we could never figure out. We kept him busy washing our clothes. We taught the houseboy how to say, "Pass the biscuits, Pappy." I wish that I could have been there when Phillips and Heising came back. I know that the houseboy will show his knowledge of the English language immediately by saying, "Pass the biscuits, Pappy." But I'm glad we were not there when they got back to find that we had been eating their food, working their servants, living in their apartment, and wearing their clothes. We are going to make it O.K. by sending them some money as soon as we hear from them. In the meantime we think we have played a good joke on them.

Javanese make excellent servants. I would like to bring a couple back. They are clean, patient, tireless workers, honest, do not drink, and particularly adapted to be house servants. However, I believe they would be as anxious to get back to the Indies as I am to get back to the U.S.

The boat trip from Batavia to Singapore was uneventful except for a little excitement one night regarding the identity of another boat, which overhauled us. We were on the after-deck and behind us in the dark we could make out the shape of another boat. We changed course and put on top speed. It overtook us, however, and went right on by. It was an Australian Red Cross ship.

Singapore was mostly Chinese. When I go back to the U.S., I want to get a couple of sharkskin suits made there and some silver objects. The city is filled with Australian soldiers and sailors. The most interesting people there are the foreign correspondents, feature writers, and broadcasters.

We entered the Rangoon River on the early morning of the 12th. About 50 miles inland we finally arrived in Rangoon—48 days from the time we left San Francisco! Rangoon was a busy place with many ships and small water taxis all over the place. The water taxis are small craft with high pointed bows and sterns operated by a native, standing in the stern, operating a paddle in anything but the conventional manner—more similar to sculling than paddling. The largest buildings in the city are alongside the river. The one outstanding object was a gold-topped pagoda. The gold in it is worth several millions of dollars. It is a magnificent structure.

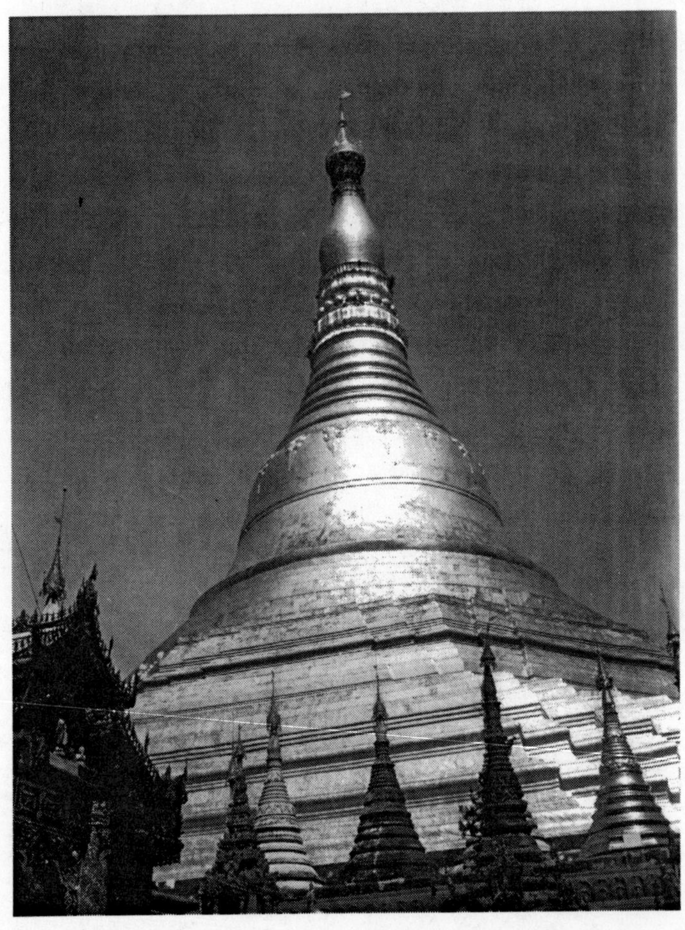

Shwedagon Pagoda, located in Yangon, the capital of Myanmar (formerly Burma).

10. HELL BENT FOR LEATHER

After getting paid for the first time since they were in California, everyone had to take half of their money—if not more, to pay their debts on the ship—especially their bar tab.

In Rangoon, they were greeted at the train station by some of the AVG pilots who had driven Studebakers down from Toungoo to pick them up. They were welcomed rather raucously, as the men had found a bar to pass the time while they waited for the train.

When they arrived at their new housing it reminded John of summer camp in his earlier years. Many of the pilots were disappointed in the less-than-stellar accommodations. In "The Flying Tigers" memoir by Russell Whelan, a radioman, he stated simply, "Toungoo was Burma at its worst." Conversely, AVG pilot Ed Rector felt like he was in Rudyard Kipling country.

Bugs and high-priced food are a bit of a gripe for John, but he has become more interested in flying and can't wait to do his part. No longer apprehensive, he is "hell bent for leather"—ready for action. However, after only being there a few days he sees there is a shortage of planes for pilot training.

The AVG was slated to receive 100 planes and 100 pilots. The ship carrying the spare parts sank before reaching Rangoon. One crate was lost over the side of the ship during unloading and had to be recovered for parts if nothing else. One of those 100 pilots, Ajax Baumler, was unable to secure a passport due to previous passport violations. So the AVG started with 99 pilots and 99 planes. The promise of more planes was never fulfilled. Without new parts available, the ground crew used parts removed from planes that had crashed and were not salvageable for flight. At times they traveled hundreds of miles to recover parts from a crash site as it was the only way to keep other planes flying.

November 16, 1941 Toungoo, Burma
Headquarters
First American Volunteer Group
Sunday

Dear Folks,

There was some partying when we left the ship. It was akin to leaving home. We had been with the other passengers and crew so long that everyone was well acquainted. It is my guess that the ship will be like a "ghost ship" during the remainder of its voyage to Calcutta. The officers and crew will long remember the American pilots they took to Rangoon. To most other people, Americans are lively, inquisitive, friendly, and forward. In Singapore we asked the clerk of the Raffles Hotel there a question about the city, and he answered with, "You will also want to know the population, height of the tallest building, the principal industry, etc., etc., you Americans always do." He was about right, at that! The English and the Dutch will take a long time to meet someone and an American will just walk right up and introduce himself!

After leaving the ship at Rangoon we went to the offices

of the Intercontinental Corp., of which the Central Aircraft Mfg. Co. is a subsidiary, and got paid. We were so broke that it took half of our first month's salary to pay our debts to the Boschfontein. Some of the guys were not so fortunate and had no money left at all.

We rode the evening train to Toungoo, which is about 150 miles north of Rangoon. This was without a doubt the worst train ride that I ever experienced in my life. Again the tracks were narrow gauge affairs and though we rode first class (all trains have 1, 2, 3, class accommodations) it was a wonder to us how the train managed to stay on the track as we could hardly stay in our seats. Four of us had a complete coach to ourselves. We tried a little poker playing, but the coins bounced up and down on the table so much that we finally gave it up. We had been paid in Burma money. The exchange rate is 3.28 for an American dollar. A rupee is similar to our dollar–16 annas make one rupee and 12 pies make one anna.

When we arrived in Toungoo all the guys were there to greet us. Gee, I was surprised at the number of fellows that were here because I didn't know that they were. What I'm trying to say is, over the din of the guys howling to get a baseball game started–is that I was surprised that so many fellows were already here. There were about 55 already here. The first bunch got here about August 15. Most of them have arrived within the past six weeks. Counting our bunch of 25 that makes a total of 80 pilots here now. So many of the planes have been cracked up that there are only about half that number of planes now. However, new ones are coming in every day. I'm sure that our bunch will crack up our share of planes. There are over 80 planes, but there are so many out of commission on account of spare parts, tires, etc. It is very difficult to set up an American organization in this part of the world. Spare parts are absolutely unavailable.

Common articles that we buy easily from our corner drug store are not to be found here. When I said that an American standard of living would cost more here, I change now to say that an American standard of living can't be maintained here–at any cost.

What I write now is November 17.

I did not fly today but will tomorrow. One of our bunch took up a P-40 today and had to land it in a rice field about 5 miles from the air-field, wheels up. He was not hurt. The others who flew for the first time today got up and down ok but were plenty nervous. Experience out here has proved that you are either not hurt at all in accidents or you are completely.

We rise at 5:30 a.m. (It seems like the middle of the night.) Breakfast at 6. As we come out from breakfast the sun is not yet visible above the mountains, but those magnificent colors that usually accompany a gorgeous sunset have the entire Eastern sky alight in a more colorful manner than I have ever witnessed in a sunrise. The most beautiful sunrises that I have ever seen before were at Fort McClellan near Anniston, Alabama. At 6:30 we are at the Squadron. There is one flying field. The Group, as the entire organization is known, is composed of 3 squadrons. These three squadrons compose The First Group–known officially as The First American Volunteer Group. Others who come over will form the Second American Volunteer Group.

We have no hangars, and the whole place looks like anything but Pensacola NAS. It reminds me more than anything of old Camp Rotary. Every building here is built of teak wood, bamboo, and rice straw. The floor and framework is teak wood. The walls are made of woven strips of flat bamboo rafters. I just called the boy (all servant boys are called boys–and when we want something done you should hear us call–Boy! Oh

Boy!!! They usually come running and say Yessie Misser). Anyway, he says the roof is made of jungle straw, which is pulled from the jungle bamboo like pulling fodder from corn stalks.

So far, I have developed two major gripes. The first gripe is really not a gripe but a disappointment. The field where we live and fly is located about eight miles from the native village of Toungoo. There is not a single white man in the town. I started to say not a single white man or woman–but we have given up hope of seeing any white women for a long time. Anyway, there is nothing to do in the town. We have twelve different movies here a month. Each movie shows for two nights. What I am trying to say is that there is not a single piece of screen in this part of the country, and if you turn on a light at night there is immediately a swarm of a million or so insects of varying descriptions that descend. Consequently it is impossible to read or write at night. That leaves the choice of going to the show or going to bed. If only we had some screen so we could screen any of a number of buildings available so we could read, write, or play cards at night. Our beds have mosquito netting canopies which keep out the bugs pretty good. These bugs wait until night before coming out. If you drive your bike down the road at night it feels like an automatic BB gun popping at you. The weather is nice and cool at night, and you have to sleep under a heavy blanket.

The next gripe is about the food. Not so much because the food is not very good as because every one of us knows darned well that we are being "rooked." We have to pay 124 rupees a month, or about $40.25 American. The guy who has the contract is a Greek and has almost a monopoly on the sources of supply around here. He is really making a cleaning on us. The whole outfit paid him $5,000 American last month, and we invariably have cabbage and potatoes at every meal along with some kind of meat. I, and I believe the rest of the guys are the same, could stand the food if we knew it was necessary. Needless to say, the Greek never shows up, but always sends some representative. We are waiting for the day when he does. We have already boycotted his Canteen which charges twice as much as stores in town for similar articles.

This would not be a real American outfit if we didn't have some gripes. I like it here very much. As much as I could like being away from home. I have taken more interest in flying than ever before. Most of us are pretty well excited about our mission and aim to do our part to down the Axis partners. The most interesting talk of the day is about scores in dive-bombing, scores in strafing, runs on a target, etc.

I will be frank about one transition in my attitude that I have noticed. Before I arrived here I had my moments of apprehension about the dangers involved. Now, I have no such apprehension. If an opportunity comes to engage the enemy, I will be hell bent for leather to do it. Now that we have arrived at what might be called "the front," we are anxious to get action. I don't think that this is just being foolhardy, it seems that when you get near where danger is, you want to do something to relieve the danger.

We will probably move up to China next week. The entire First Group will move up together. A great deal of the supplies, etc., are already there. As a matter of fact, it was first planned to have the pilots go there right away upon arriving in Rangoon.

John next to a Tomahawk and China Air Force 12 point roundel.
National Naval Aviation Museum collection

11. WE OUGHT TO BE RUGGED AFTER A YEAR LIKE THIS

John is having second thoughts about how newsworthy a month-old *Time* magazine will be when he finally receives it overseas. He suggests his mother use her address for the subscription.

Again, he explains what should be written on the envelope to get mail to him in a timely manner.

John asks his mother to show his letters to Gould Beech, John's friend and an award-winning journalist, to see if Gould "is interested in any of the stuff that I write." John had worked with Beech at the Montgomery Advisor newspaper and valued his work. It's as if John intended all along for more people to read about his experience.

Most of this letter is typed "with the typewriter on my knees sitting on another fellow's bed who has rigged up a light," but John adds a chilling handwritten postscript. "If you have any apprehension concerning my having been killed…call CAMCO."

All of the First American Volunteer Group are now together. John's group aboard the Boschfontein was the last to arrive. They have 3 squadrons: the 1st Pursuit Squadron is The Adam and Eves, 2nd Pursuit Squadron is The Panda Bears, and John is assigned to the 3rd Pursuit Squadron, The Hell's Angels. The plan had been for each squadron to have 33 planes, but by the time John arrives several planes were already lost due to accidents.

Unbeknown to most of the world, a cable to President Roosevelt was sent—but ignored. Joseph Clark Grew, American ambassador to Japan, sent a telegram to Washington warning, "There is a lot of talk around town to the effect that the Japanese, in case of a break with the United States, are planning to go all out in a surprise mass attack on Pearl Harbor."

Nov. 18, 1941
Box 2000
Rangoon, Burma

Dearest Folks,

I have received no letters from you all. If you don't want to spend the 70¢ for air mail, then send the letter air mail to Honolulu which costs 20¢ and by boat from there. Mark the letter "Air-mail to Honolulu–boat from there." One of the fellows received several letters from the States in 18 days that were sent thusly. What happened was that the letters stayed on the Clipper all the way.

We are having a wonderful experience. I write this in our barracks, which consist of a barn-like structure with a row of bunks on each side and an aisle between. It is practically like camping out. We ought to be rugged after a year like this. We only work half days–from 6 until noon. In the afternoons we write, read, play baseball, volleyball, go on hikes, etc.

How is everyone at home? Is Wayne growing to be a big guy? This letter should reach you before Xmas. I am sorry that I won't be able to present presents, but let Mamma write some checks and I wish you all a very merry Xmas and a happy New Year. Give Bobby something for me. Last Xmas he brought me a present, and I had forgotten to get one for him. If James is in school Mamma, be sure to help him out financially. And don't forget to get something nice for yourself too, Mamma.

Did you hear from Time magazine in regard to the subscription that I sent them? I now find it takes so long for a copy to get here by boat that it would be of little news value. If you like you can have the subscription changed to your address.

Also, you might deposit by check another $500 in the Southern California Building and Loan Association, or make the total in this bank an even $1000. Also, I believe that it would be best to keep $500 in the checking account with the Union Bank and Trust Co., in case that I or you may need to write a check sometime. So far, I have had no need to write a check, but I might have to. If you wish to buy more U.S. Savings Bonds, it might be a good idea.

With a monthly salary of $75 and out of this $40 for mess bill, $3 for laundry, $6.70 for insurance, $5 for club dues, etc., there won't be much left. Fortunately, there aren't many places to spend money, but some of the things that you might want like film, soft drinks, shorts, etc., cost like the deuce, also stamps. By the way, how do you like the stamps on the envelope?

I am having this letter registered. At least this way the censors won't throw it away. I wish I knew exactly what they cut out, if anything, and how they do it. If any letters from me are censored tell me what letter and what paragraph, i.e., what preceded the sentence or paragraph that was cut out. Also, tell me what date you receive them. Certainly you must have written—yet, I have received only two letters since I have been here. Both of these were from Sybil and if anybody is not in position to buy air mail stamps—it's Sybil. She is making her own way in L.A. and trying to go to school in addition. In her last letter she said that she had a job with Bell Telephone Co. and that she had a chance of getting transferred to Honolulu and that she might go there.

Let me know if Gould is interested in any of the stuff I write. I don't have enough time to go over it or put it in an orderly manner. It must read like something terrible.

There is a lot of information that I could give a guy coming over in regard to what to bring, etc. I wish that I had brought some flight gear—particularly a pair of goggles. However, I will get along ok on what I have, I hope.

I am writing this at night with the typewriter on my knees sitting on another fellow's bed who has rigged up a light. The canopy of mosquito netting is all around the bed and extends about 5 feet above the bed. I have arranged with him that he goes to the movie the first night the show is shown, and I will use his bunk and light, then I go the second night and he can use my typewriter. We never worry about what is on—we go whether we have seen it a dozen times before or not.

This position is so uncomfortable that I will have to cease trying and finish tomorrow afternoon. Good night. The stars are out in all their glory tonight, and it is nice and cool.

It is now Saturday Nov. 22. I have been laid up in the hospital for several days with tonsillitis. I have not received a letter from anyone but Sybil, yet. When you have read this letter, i.e., the other five pages, first call Gould and see if he wants to read it. After he finishes with it, write Sybil and ask if she has received a carbon copy of the letter. If she has not then you can send it to her to read. Of course I don't mean to send this page. In case some of my mail is held up, I am requesting Sybil to let you know when she hears from me. Since regular mail (boat mail) takes so long, it is hardly worth-while to send it that way.

If you address mail to Box 2000 in addition to the address, the censors will get at it right away.

I received a cablegram from Olyn Gragg. He is in Melbourne, England. He wanted to come over here, but I'm sure that they would only want service men here. He was flying Bombers to Britain.

If this weighs too much to get it in the other letter I will send it separate.

Love,
John

P.S. If at any time you have any apprehension concerning me or hear any rumors concerning my having been killed, etc., (some fellows here receive some of the most awful letters telling them that they had heard they had been killed) call collect, Central Aircraft Manufacturing Company, 30 Rockefeller Plaza, New York City. Ask to speak to Mr. Brown or Lt. Commander Irvine. If they don't know anything they will cable over here and find out and call you back. But if anything should happen to me, I think you would be notified. However, if as I said–you have any apprehension at all–then call CAMCO New York.

John's caption reads: "American pilots, Chinese planes, & British territory."
National Naval Aviation Museum collection

12. THE ROAD TO MANDALAY

When John's mother receives this letter, it reflects the censoring he has mentioned so many times.

Censoring was not new and dates back to the Civil War. When soldiers informed their family where they were and what unit they were with, that information would be blacked out or the entire letter was confiscated.

The censor's duty was to cut or black out anything that would give the enemy anything of value. "Loose lips sink ships" was a popular phrase during World War II. The soldier or airman's location or what they were doing was bound to be blacked out. Anything that would cast weakness would be removed. Soldier morale was monitored.

Censorship during the Korean War (1950-1953) was minimal and non-existent during the Vietnam War (1955-1975). Toward the end of the Vietnam War the military didn't even bother to cancel (postmarked FREE during wars) the letters.

In today's world, censorship takes a different form. Our military living in war zones with Internet access will experience temporary lapses in Internet connections prior to missions. This is to prevent intelligence from being intercepted. Another reason for a temporary outage involves casualty notifications. It is mandatory that next-of-kin notification protocol be followed—and not leaked to social media.

First American Volunteer Group
Toungoo, Burma

November 25, 1941

Dear Folks,

We are busily engaged in the many necessary tasks to maintain and improve a Pursuit Group that may at any time be called upon to engage the enemy. This is a man-size job. Especially is it true here where equipment is limited and spare parts unheard of. Fortunately, Trans-Pacific Clipper is bringing in a few tires and propellers, which are sorely needed. Gun sights and radios have to be improvised to fit our planes.

I heard that parts of Burma were rough and wild. After flying over the area around here I can easily believe that. There are tigers, bison, elephants, king cobras, and multitudes of monkeys. Several fellows have monkeys for pets. Monkeys can be bought in any quantity for 2 or 3 dollars each.

On the range of mountains to the North, elephants are used to haul teak trees out of the forest to the road. When I flew over there today, I noticed that they had quit work. I found out later that the elephants won't work in the heat of the day. When I was over the place before it was about 8 in the morning. Apparently elephants have a pretty strong union up there and refuse to work from about 10 in the morning until 4 in the afternoon. If I get a chance, I will go up there by the road. I understand that wild elephants here are easy to tame—much more so than their African brothers.

Yesterday I saw a snake charmer at work. We were in nearby Toungoo cycling along the "main street" when we heard the tom-tom of a drum and saw a crowd gathered. The snake charmer had several acts to his show. He had a boy from the audience (all of us guessed that the boy was his own son) come out and then he proceeded to perform antics and emit noises, which were to hypnotize the lad. This done, the snake charmer put a king cobra in the boy's clothing and left it there during the rest of the performance. There followed a lot of antics with the other cobras, which was rather frightening considering that this snake is more deadly than a rattlesnake. The performer played his flute while the cobra would rear up and strike at him. These snakes are shaped like other snakes, these were 6 to 10 feet long, but when they become angry their heads flatten out. They only strike downwards and then they are surprisingly slow. This fellow sure had the word on how to handle cobras, but for myself, I want no part of them.

I suppose the most romantic of the things here is the moon over Burma, which we have every night and the road to Mandalay, which passes right outside our camp.

I have never learned to carry a tune. This is not true because I always carry a tune around with me. I usually whistle it because I cannot sing in tune, try as I might. The nearest that I ever came to learning how to sing a song was in Chicago when a singing teacher tried for two months to teach me how to sing a song without completely murdering it. The song that we most frequently worked on was "The Road to Mandalay." Because I reached a modicum of success at singing it, this has been one of my favored songs. Now when I turn out of camp and hit the road to Mandalay, I break out in this song. Yesterday I had my picture taken standing beneath a road sign. One of the arrows pointing South read "To Rangoon," the other pointing North read "To Mandalay." This picture I will keep for a long time.

Last night six more pilots, all former Navy, and eight mechanics arrived. I believe that we have as fine a bunch of pilots and mechanics as could be gotten together. Never have I seen a better spirit of group solidarity than here. The Group is very lax as far as military discipline is concerned. Individuality is given freedom. Some of the fellows have not shaved for over a month. Others are growing the weirdest beards, goatees, sideburns, and mustaches imaginable. Uniform regulations are practically nil. There is no saluting, marching, or military procedure of any kind. Everyone realizes that there is a task to be done. Everyone is trying their best to perform this task. I believe that the Group is more efficient here than it would be in the Navy or Army. I have seen mechanics work twelve hours a day here and be happy in their accomplishments during that time. Of course, this happens infrequently as we work only until noon, having the time from then until 6:30 the next morning free. Real ability is the first measurement of a man's worth here.

This afternoon "C" Squadron pilots won the baseball game from "A" Squadron men. This keeps us leading the league with 6 games won and 0 games lost. We should win the trophy Col. Chennault is offering to the League winner.

The name of the pagoda in Rangoon that is so famous is Shwedagon. There are over 3000 Buddhas within the pagoda. One of these is richly adorned with precious jewels. The roof is entirely of gold leaf. When the people come to worship, and many come far distances to worship at this famous shrine, they leave gifts. The rich give gold, jewels, money, and the poorest cut the longest strands of hair from their head, which they leave. Buddha was supposed to have been 85 feet tall. An impression of his footprints is in the floor of the pagoda, which is very old, first built about 2500 years ago. It is quite a contrast to be in some sections of the city where the natives live in squalid thatch one-room huts without benefit of sanitation, running water, electricity, with food scarce, and what food there is covered with flies, bugs, mosquitoes, and look out toward the business section of

Rangoon and see this lofty gold-covered pagoda rising above other buildings of the city.

Today is Thanksgiving—November 27. We maintained our usual flying schedule. For lunch we had turkey and dressing, but there was no cranberry sauce. The meal was one of the best that we have had in some time. Of course today is no holiday here in Burma.

Looking at the desk calendar I see that for the Burmese this is the 10th waxing of Nadaw 1303. The front of the calendar says that it is published by the Yomah club. At the top of each page are the English and Burmese dates. At the bottom is a quotation together with the person's name who submitted it. For today the quotation is, "He is not worthy to live at all that for the fear of death, shunneth his country's service and his honour." By Sir Humphrey Gilbert. Here is some more from the front of the calendar: "The year 1941 will be a momentous one in the history of nations. Our duty is plain. 'When the ruthless ambitions of a man threaten to engulf the world, it becomes the solemn obligation of free men, wherever they may be, to affirm that the world belongs not to any man, but to all men, and that freedom is the deed and title to the soil on which we exist.'" Queen Elizabeth of Spain. The Burmese year began on the 5th waxing of Hnaung Tagu or 15th April, 1941. The calendar months are based on the moon.

Glancing through some of the other quotations I noticed that they range from questions from Mary Baker Eddy, Shakespeare, Wordsworth, Lloyd George, Shelley, Reader's Digest, etc. This one appears for the 12th waxing of Pyatho 1302 or January 8, 1941: "A Negro railway porter in America on the trouble with the world: 'The trouble is, that everybody's goin' into the barber business; everybody wants to shave the other fellow, and he's got a beard his'self,' Anonymous."

I think the Negro has something there. The thanks for this

quotation was given to Mrs. Leonard B. Allen, Judson College, Rangoon. It sure would be swell if the Judson College that I know were down in Rangoon. That would give us something to do with our evenings, and I bet all of us would be there every evening.

Charles Dickens has a good thought for today. "Reflect upon your present blessing of which every man has many—not on your misfortunes, of which all men have some."

Not having had a glass of milk since September 24th, I can think of nothing better to eat today than two or three gallons of ice-cold sweet milk.

Air mail letters take from 15-20 days to arrive here. The censors have promised that if the mail is addressed to Box 2000, Rangoon, Burma, it will be inspected without delay. The distribution of the mail is one of the biggest events of the day here.

Our chutes are Chinese-made but are very similar to U.S. Navy type. They have worked successfully in the instances in which they have been used.

Nearly everyone wears 12" fighter boots, which are handmade in of our own design and purchased to order for 22 to 24 rupees. The boot-makers do an excellent job, but the leather is not cured as well as in the U.S. I think that typifies most of the articles made here. Despite the fact that most things are handmade, yet cheaper—they still are not up to American standards. The U.S. certainly has the jump on these countries out here when it comes to the quantity and quality of manufactured articles—anything from toothpaste to airplanes. One cannot realize what an industrialized nation the U.S. is until some of these countries are seen. At home we take for granted hundreds of things that over here are considered priceless luxuries. Right now—boy, what I wouldn't give for a Coca-Cola.

Every night we have a camp paper, which is mimeographed and contains highlights of the world news. This keeps us abreast of the Japanese situation anyway, but as far as other news is concerned there is very little.

Did I tell you about the bicycles here? Everyone has a bicycle. The buildings are so scattered that they are a virtual necessity. We bought ours in Singapore and brought them up with us on the boat. Lucky thing, too, because bicycles are much higher here. They are still higher in China. An odd thing about bicycles here is that they have no roller coaster brakes. By this I mean that when you put on brakes in the American way, there aren't any. You can be coasting forward and turning the pedals in reverse. Braking is accomplished by means of hand grips attached to the handlebars which press rubber grips against the front and rear rims. The bicycles are made in England. American bicycles are much better, but like American cigarettes they are probably illegal to import. I can see now that colonies are convenient things to have to sell goods to. I still believe that the U.S. should go in for more colonies.

Guns and ammunition are practically impossible to purchase. I wish that I had brought along a rifle and pistol. As it is, the only firing I do is maneuvering the airplane toward a target and blazing away with fixed machine guns. Enough of the fellows have guns that I can borrow one to go hunting with.

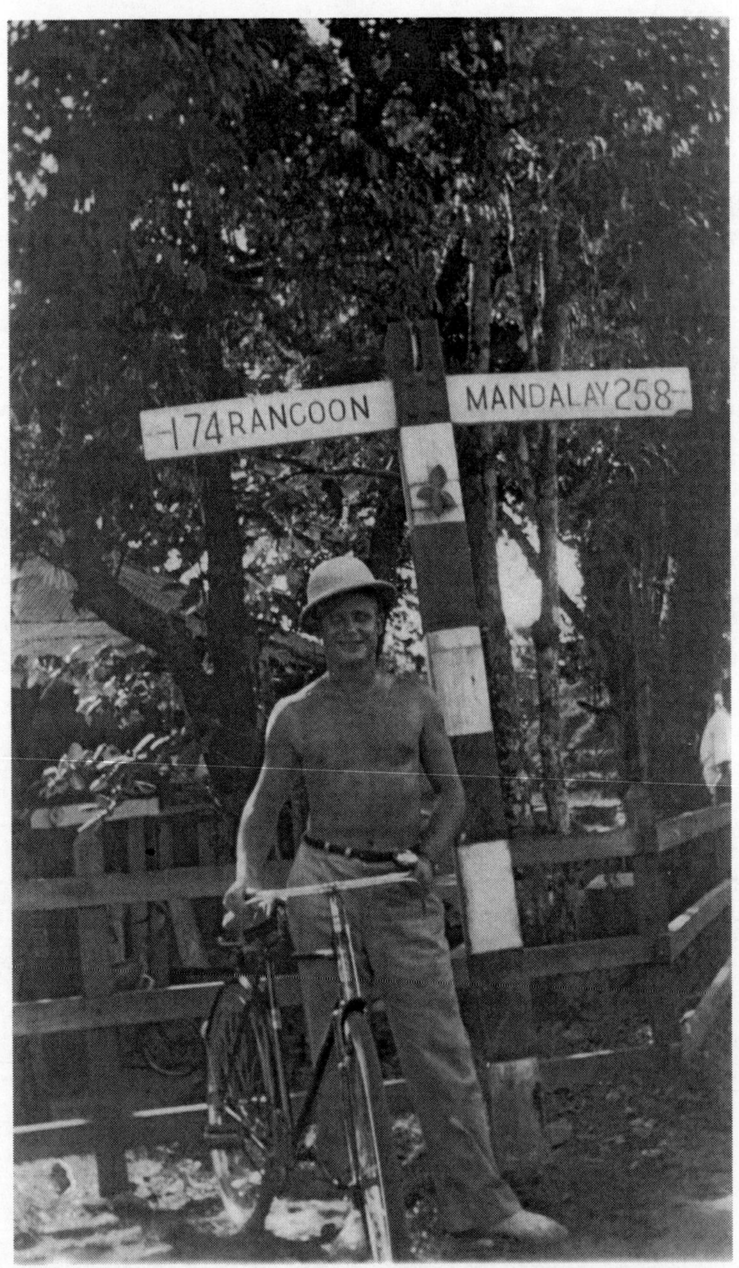

"This picture I will keep for a long time."
John's caption
National Naval Aviation Museum collection

Snake Charmer (John's caption)
National Naval Aviation Museum collection

13. PEARL HARBOR

"Today they have gone and done it!" John exclaims. News that Pearl Harbor had been bombed spread quickly through the Group via Japanese radio broadcast. Chennault immediately requests the AVG be moved from their present location of Toungoo, Burma, because they were too close to the border of Thailand where the Japanese planes enter Burma. Madame Chiang Kai-shek gave approval for a move to Yunnan, more than 900 miles away, but two days later, her husband, the Generalissimo, ordered the group to stay. Chennault then sent John's squadron, the Hell's Angels, to Rangoon's Mingaladon Field. (John's letter is not dated December 7th, because he was across the International Date Line.) The United States and Britain declare war on Japan.

December 8, 1941

Well, today they have gone and done it. You have to give the guys credit for nerve. Today and for many days to come there will be changes made. We received the news this morning. It was hard to believe. We don't know yet what the facts are, but we wonder what the fellows were doing at Pearl Harbor to let the Japs sneak up on them. Somebody apparently was asleep. Knowing my own weaknesses and shortcomings and realizing that the safety of a place like Hawaii is dependent upon the watchfulness, bravery, and ability of guys like myself—many of the fellows at Pearl Harbor were in my class at Pensacola—I can see how it could have happened. Yet, the Japs should never have gotten within a thousand miles of Hawaii. Where were all those "P" boat pilots who are supposed to maintain a lookout constantly within a 600-mile circle surrounding Hawaii? Now that the Navy guys are awake, they will probably give the Japs hell.

It should never have happened. A big country like the U.S., standing by, completely trying to conciliate the murderers. Yes, that's the trouble with a fine democracy showing too much kindness to the wrong people. While we are trying to maintain the peace we let them get in a sock to our jaw. This goes to support my aggressive peace policy. It should never have happened because we knew it was going to happen. Knowing that it was going to happen, we should have kicked them in the pants first—then it probably never would have happened. By following an aggressive peace policy, at least you aren't taken by surprise—you start the affair when you are ready, instead of having it started for you when you aren't ready.

Now that the war is on, I imagine the British censorship will be even more strict. For this reason and because of the dangers involved, I will not be able to write about our own activities, lest this should get in the wrong hands.

When this letter will get to the States is another question. Probably it might be routed out of Australia or around the other way.

We have only heard incomplete and unconfirmed accounts of the first few hours of the war. As I have said, our first news that Pearl Harbor had been bombed was almost unbelievable. We had a better impression of our Navy guys there. Apparently someone, or a lot of people, was sleeping. We have laughed at some of the countries in Europe for being caught napping—now we have been caught in the same act. We haven't given the British much credit, but the news says that the attack on Singapore was repulsed. You have to give the Tommies credit for being on the alert. I spent the weekend in Rangoon. All week Burma has been observing blacked-out regulations every night. Rangoon was the blackest black-out that I have ever seen. Riding around in the rickshaws and taxis is risky business at night, yet the natives seem to have some uncanny second nature which shows them the way from place to place.

Japan's attack on the U.S. probably doesn't surprise us over here as much as the people at home. Over here we know that the Japs are aggressive militarists. The thing that surprised us was that she got the jump on the U.S. It probably amounts to our being surprised at the U.S. for waiting so long and then being surprised. Over here we are always on the alert for the Japanese offensives. It has been going on over here for four years. However, one always feels that he is different or that his country is different. America has probably thought 'surely Japan won't attack us, no, not us.' Alas, they have and now when America realizes that the war has come home they will get ready to fight.

We Americans over here will give a good account of ourselves because war has been on our doorsteps ever since we've been here. We are psychologically, physically, and technically ready to fight the enemy. These things make an awful lot of difference in any military outfit. Many soldiers, sailors, aviators who have been in the Army, Navy, or Air Corps for years have learned the theoretical principles and methods of warfare but have never thought in their own mind that they may have to risk their neck someday. As long as there is no real danger—danger itself seems unreal—one goes along lackadaisical—then when real danger threatens, it takes a moment to realize what it is and the risks involved and another moment to get into the aforementioned psychological, physical state to combat it. I dare say that few, if any, were aware of the danger involved immediately before the bombing of Hawaii—else how did it happen? It is going to be interesting to find out how the Japs got there without being seen. Over here we have known danger was at hand—I doubt if they could have pulled such a stunt on us.

Maybe so—

With it all a fellow has to eat and it's chow time—so goodbye until later.

14. WAR IS BIG BUSINESS

In this letter John mentions Senator Burton K. Wheeler who served in Congress 1923-1947. Wheeler had been opposed to war and had been quoted as saying, "If we did [go to war], it would only be to help the British." When the Japanese bombed Pearl Harbor, the Senator changed his mind and was all in.

One member of the Group quit (dishonorable discharge) and went to board a ship to return to the States. Although John gave him a few things to take back to his family, John was expecting the quitter to have to return to the AVG, as the ship would more than likely be stuck in port now that war had been declared.

The bombing of Pearl Harbor was devastating. In less than two hours, 353 Japanese airplanes bombed and strafed the harbor and base, causing 2,403 casualties, including 68 civilians. Japan's calculated early-morning attack also injured 1,178 military and civilians. Twenty-three sets of brothers died aboard the USS Arizona, as well as a father and son. The entire unit of the NBU-22, a Navy military band, were all killed-in-action.

December 9

This is another day. As if getting up at 5:30 isn't early enough, we now arise at 4 and remain on the alert all day with the exception of the night crew, whose jobs are performed at night.

We have heard that when Senator Wheeler was notified that the Japs had bombed Pearl Harbor he said, "This means war." This has been a laughing matter with the entire group ever since we heard it. Sometimes it takes something like this to make some people realize that other nations do not always respect the integrity and peace of other nations. Our group has already been at war with the Japanese. Our planes have the Chinese insignia on both wings.

When I look back and read paragraphs like the above, I am struck with the fact that my English, sentence structure, etc. isn't as good as it was when I used to be in 3rd grade.

There are now few areas in the world not touched by war. Tibet is one of them. If too many enemy planes get after me, I will head west. There would be no place to land among those mountains over there, however, so I would have to bail out. They probably haven't heard of parachute troops so they wouldn't shoot me. I could live the rest of my life there and probably never hear another word about the outside world–this would only be true in the most remote and highest mountain areas.

But we have better ways of handling a situation like this. When too many enemy planes get after one of us we dive down over an area where we have strong anti-aircraft batteries. The gunners recognize our planes and let us by–when the enemy plane comes along all the gunners let them have hot lead. Since this probably isn't an original idea, I don't think the censors will cut this out.

What our status will be now that the U.S. is at war, we do not know. I imagine that we will continue as before, i.e. to carry on our work here.

I would say that the greatest single advantage in warfare

is the element of surprise. This is what the Japs pulled on America. I wouldn't be the least surprised if most of the planes at Pearl Harbor did not have camera guns mounted in them. They were probably proud that on a few hours' notice they would be ready for combat. As I understand the news, they didn't have any warning. If the Japs could have gotten into the U.S. proper they would have caught many a military unit asleep. Having served in the Navy myself, I know that it is very possible to over-rate our own state of preparedness. I still say that it should never have happened. We should not have been caught napping. Inasmuch as we were aware of the presence of the danger for several years we still continued a policy that allowed ourselves to be attacked. This is the fault of the Government's policy. Some military and Naval units are probably very embarrassed today that they allowed the enemy to slip up on them.

This morning we are maintaining patrols at all levels. Jap land troops are moving in closer. If anything, the U.S. being involved in the war will probably relieve pressure of Jap attacks upon us as their forces will be engaged in many other points, which will be of more importance to them. Most of us are itching for a good fight with them—especially now that we realize that they have attacked the U.S.—the chance might come today or tomorrow.

I do not know why I write this as it will be a month or months before this reaches home, and by then the situation will be so changed that this will be old stuff and our own situation over here will have been altered considerably.

Enough of the war. In Rangoon I purchased a few items of clothing and saw a fairly recent movie, also went through the Shwe Pagoda. Wearing of footwear is not allowed inside so you leave your shoes and socks on the steps. Also went aboard an American ship, which was in port. Oh yes, one of our fellows was going back to the States on this ship. Now he will probably come back with the Group as it is likely that the ship will be tied up here, maybe. He was going to carry back a few things for me, too—now I guess that will have to wait until I get back.

War is the biggest business in the world today, and yet, fundamentally war doesn't have a leg to stand on when considered in respect to the good that it accomplishes. Yet it is probably one of the few things that will always be with us.

15. BURMA

Germany and Italy declared war on the United States December 11, 1941. The U.S. reciprocated and declared war against Germany and Italy.

For the first time in U.S. history—perhaps the only time—every citizen was behind the war effort. War production profoundly changed American industry. New car manufacturing came to a standstill. Following the bombing of Pearl Harbor, only 138 new cars were made, and the production lines stopped until the end of the war. The car plant facilities were redesigned to make whatever was needed for tanks and planes. Detroit was nicknamed the Arsenal of Democracy.

Nylon stocking production ceased, and DuPont made ropes and parachutes instead. The war in the Pacific cut off the supply of rubber for tires. Kids collected scrap metal, and families bought war bonds to support the war effort. Life had changed for everyone.

John is frank about the Japanese being resourceful and determined—and that everyone underestimated them. Censors removed his whereabouts in this letter.

Now that war is affecting people at home, John asks about his brother, James—and hopes he won't have to enlist.

██████ Burma December 10 ██████████

Dearest Folks,

The complexion of world events has taken a change and

now the U.S. is at war. I hope that there will be no undue hardships on any of you. What is James doing now? I wish that he were employed in some defense job that will free him from the responsibility of joining the Army or Navy.

Over here all of us are well and happy as could be considering that we are so far from home. We are well trained and able to give good account of ourselves when the time comes. You need have no worry about me as compared to the natives around here; we live like kings and have plenty of servants who call us "Mawster" and "Sahib." Our position is much less dangerous now that the Japanese have scattered their forces from the shores of America to Siam.

I have written a couple of checks totaling about 200 dollars or more on the Union bank. These were for some jewelry and cashmere silk, which I wish to bring back as presents. One of the boys was scheduled to leave yesterday from Rangoon to go back to the States, and he had the package with him. Now that the war is in the Pacific, I imagine he will be back up here with us in a few days. So I will keep the stuff until I find some other way or come back myself. There was a beautiful sapphire and zircon bracelet and sapphire and diamond ring, along with some hand-made embroidered cashmere pieces, including a bedspread and table cover for you–and something nice for Mary Ellen.

We managed to get the Singapore and London radio stations as well as some in China, but not yet have we heard any news from any station in the States. I imagine the attack by the Japs rather startled everyone to say the least. I know that it is easy for the U.S. to overestimate their own state of preparedness. They are fighting a determined and resourceful enemy who is well versed in all the methods of modern warfare. We underrated the Japs and they pulled a fast one. I am convinced that they will have to pay dearly in the long run, but in the meantime they have caused considerable damage which could have been entirely avoided had we been more positive with them and less lenient.

I do not say that the Japs don't have causes for their aggression; but I do say that these causes are not sufficient and for their thinking so they will bloody well find out how wrong they were.

When and if this letter reaches you is doubtful. I believe it will, but will probably take more time than heretofore.

In one of my letters I suggested some things to do with the funds in our account. These were just suggestions, if you have any need for the money other than what was suggested, then use it for whatever you please. If you don't, then I think that the bank and Federal Savings Bonds are the best things. For myself I am still getting along ok on the $75 dollars a month, but for things to bring back I will have to write checks on the checking account–for this reason, I think that it is a good idea to keep at least a $500 dollar balance in this account at the Union Bank.

So far I have received only one letter from you. That means that I was here almost one month before hearing from you all. You should not have waited so long to let me receive word as I was worried. Your letter was mailed in Montgomery about October 4 and arrived here about December 6. Air mail is about the only satisfactory means of writing.

We are taking it pretty easy today.

Love, John

3rd Pursuit Squadron The Hells Angels
John Donovan standing second from the left
National Naval Aviation Museum collection

16. CHRISTMAS HAS COME AND GONE

In this letter dated December 28th, 1941, John writes about Christmas coming and going, the first air-to-air combat, and how the AVG has suffered their first personnel loss. John continues writing on January 1st after moving to Kunming, as the Japanese had aggressively run the 3rd Squadron north. John hasn't seen combat yet—due to a continued shortage of planes. The pilots who have, though, are giving him a good idea of what it is like.

Mail was slow with censors holding it up for weeks. If too much of the letter was censored it was disposed of. Later on, in 1944, V-letters (V for victory) were used to speed up the process of getting correspondence from home. V-letters were stationery and envelope, all-in-one. The small, standardized size quickly went through mail sorting centers. As the letter passed through military post office censoring it was microfilmed and reduced in size, and expedited overseas. There wasn't much room to write, but the letters went from sender to recipient much quicker than in the AVG days of '41 and '42.

The move to Kunming was supported by CNAC, China National Aviation Corporation. CNAC was a commercial airline company best known for flying rescues during the first few days following the bombing of Pearl Harbor. They also flew cargo over "The Hump" during the war. The Hump was named by Allied pilots and was a dangerous 530 mile route over the Himalayan mountain range which was crucial for resupplying for the war. This company was jointly owned by the Chinese government and Pan Am Airlines and had Chinese and American pilots. John gives great credit to the skill of the pilots of CNAC.

Talks of inducting the AVG into the military began to spread. The men's reaction was nothing short of resentment. Chennault was making every effort to salvage the AVG under the original plan. Madame Chiang Kai-shek began communications with Washington about induction of personnel who chose to remain. She specifically requested Col. Chennault to stay and command whatever military unit was sent from the United States.

Chennault was ill on numerous occasions, which John mentions in several letters. In this particular letter he refers to the Chaplain as "Joe" being the caregiver to the ailing commander. The AVG nicknamed Chaplin Paul Frillman as "Holy Joe."

Chronic bronchitis plagued him for the rest of his life. He died of lung cancer on July 27, 1958, in New Orleans, Louisiana, at the Oshsner Clinic. Claire Chennault is buried in Section 2 of Arlington National Cemetery. His headstone is in both English and Chinese.

December 28, 1941

It has been some time since I have last written. This has been because I had hoped to hear again from home–which I have not–and mostly due to the fact that now the U.S. is in the war and it will take much longer to get mail through now than before–if it gets through at all. I can say here that one certainly learns who one's friends are when they are far away by whether they hear from them or not. I have received precious few letters so I assume that I have precious few friends.

Much has happened recently. Christmas has come and gone quietly as a mouse. Christmas here was no different from any other day as every day is a work day. For example, today is Sunday but one wouldn't know it. War doesn't celebrate holidays or days of worship. However, I have read of skirmishes between opposing armies when they declare a truce for the duration of the holiday or when they agree not to fight between sun-up and sundown on Sunday. It would be nice if we could relax for one day a week. What would be nicer would be to have some kind of entertainment occasionally. Here there is absolutely nothing at all to do for amusement or diversion. This afternoon I would like to go to Toungoo and just bike around the town hollering "OK" to the natives. This is one word they all know, and they shout it to every American they see.

Our fellows have given a good account of themselves in the three encounters they have had with the Japs. The first was in Kunming December 19, when the first squadron took on 10 bombers and brought down 6. None of our fellows were hurt, and we lost no planes except the one Fritz Wolf cracked up when he made a forced landing after running out of gas. The wags have it that Newkirk made a couple passes at the bomber without having first turned his gun switch on.

The enemy was intercepted about 60 miles from Kunming. The second squadron apparently stayed above the aerodrome, protecting it.

The 3rd squadron took on about 50 bombers and 20 fighters escorting over Rangoon on December 23rd and brought down 14 enemy aircraft. We had been told to get the leader of a bomber formation and that would disrupt the others. Chuck Older dove through a whole formation and knocked down the leader but another slipped right into his place. They say that the Japs fly the tightest and best formation they have ever seen. Also, that their bombing is very accurate. Neil Martin, the guy I like best in the whole outfit and who was an A-1 athlete, was killed when his plane got in the cross fire of the bombers as he was pulling up. Hank Gilbert went down in flames. Paul Greene bailed out and the Japs shot at him all the way down but never hit him. His chute split partly upon opening, and he dropped pretty fast and hit the ground with a terrible wallop bruising him badly. The Japs lost 14 aircraft confirmed with about 22 probable.

The next flight was on Xmas when they came over again with about the same number of bombers and fighters. This time they lost 10 bombers and 9 fighters confirmed with others probable. The A.V.G. lost no fellows this time but Edmund Overend and George McMillan were missing for a couple of days. Parker Dupouy's ship had a collision with a Jap fighter. The Jap went down, but Dupouy managed to get his plane back though the wing and aileron were damaged badly. Robert Hedman has been credited with four bombers. Ralph Gunvordahl said that one of the fellows shot a fighter off Curtis Smith's tail.

Kunming January 1, 1941

Arrived here 3 a.m. the morning of December 31 by C.N.A.C. The pilot and copilot were both Chinese. You really have to hand it to the CNAC pilots. They take off, fly through the clouds skirting mountain tops and come down through overcast and they're right above the airport. We left Toungoo at 6 p.m. December 30th and arrived in Lashio at 9 p.m. It was cold as the devil there and me with a pair of khaki pants and shirt. Needless to say I almost froze. There were 10 of us on the transport, but when we arrived at Lashio there was a huge crowd of Chinese that wanted to board it. They took out all our baggage, tools, equipment, etc., and weighed it. I sure felt guilty, as all of us must have. Our baggage probably averaged 100 pounds per man. They never weigh the baggage at Toungoo, and all the fellows have been getting away with murder though the limit is supposed to be 35 pounds per man. As a matter of fact, I thought, as most of us did, that the plane was chartered for our use. But when I saw all the women and children pleading for room on the ship, I was glad that we suggested to leave two huge crates that were in the baggage compartment for a later ship. As I said, when we arrived at Lashio there were 10 passengers. When we left Lashio for Kunming there were 27 passengers though there are only 21 seats. It was a DC-3, and it was fairly comfortable as about 6 of the passengers were children. Needless to say, however, we were somewhat concerned and were glad when it got off the ground before all the runway was used up. The total load limit exceeded by about 200 kilograms the ordinary load limit.

I was more concerned about the entire trip, despite my knowing that the CNAC pilots are about the best, than on any other trip in a transport before. As a matter of fact this was the first commercial transport that I have ever ridden in. All Navy transports have parachutes. This plane had none. In addition we skirted the mountain tops ominously close, and it was a rough ride throughout. I would have felt much better if an American pilot had been in charge. This is probably prejudice, but if McDonald or Sweet had been at the wheel I would have been more at ease.

Page 2 January 1, 1941

The chief pilot was a small Chinese who loved to swear American style and did it with affluence. He was an energetic chap while the other two were phlegmatic and took care of details.

I feel wonderful. It seems like Xmas. The place here is swell. It is very cold but I like it. The only present that I received this Xmas was a silk scarf from the Generalissimo. He gave these to all the pilots and men. The scarf is made of white silk and has the Chiang Kai-shek's chop on it in red embroidered silk. The chop is his signature. I think that I will keep it rather than wear it. The only Xmas card that I received was from the Ceylon-Burma Trading Corporation from whom I bought some things when one of their representatives came to Toungoo.

More reasons that this seems like Xmas. There is a big sign on the entrance to the main building that has written in cheery letters "Merry Xmas and Happy New Year" with a picture of Santa Claus on it. Upstairs in the auditorium is a Xmas tree. The day before we got here or earlier, they had a big Xmas party and dinner. But the one present, which by the way, was done up nicely in a Xmas bag, and the cold and the atmosphere is making me feel good all over and every day seems like Xmas, and I keep waiting for something good to happen.

When we arrived at the airport yesterday we were met by Bill Blackburn and three station wagons. We nearly froze until we got to Hostel number one, which is our living place. They gave us a hot meal, which was welcome and we went to bed.

The place here is the nicest building that I have seen in all of Kunming and used to be an agricultural college. From everything that I have seen, I can say that the Chinese have gone to no end of trouble or expense to do everything they could to furnish nice living quarters, sanitary conditions, recreation rooms, and excellent meals. They have certainly been nice to the group. There is a W.S.A.C. (War Service Area Corps), which cooperates in furnishing people as interpreters, guides, and liaison people for our group. They are swell!

The entire place here where we live and the offices remind me more than anything else of George Williams College. As a matter of fact that has been on my mind constantly. I actually feel like I did at George Williams. I like the climate. It certainly gives one more zip and vitality. Each pilot has a separate room. And the nicest of all things–running hot water. I have not shaved with hot water nor bathed with hot water since arriving in Rangoon Nov. 12. It is not necessary to say that when I got up and shaved with hot water I went into the showers and stood under the hot water for 45 minutes. Maybe that's what makes this place remind me of George Williams. There I used to swim lots and also at the Central YMCA and the Union League Boys Club and at all the places, I liked nothing better than to stand under a hot shower for long lengths of time with the result that I nearly always had "bath pruritus," a home-made name for itchy skin caused because of all the oil washed out of the skin.

The Col. is sick with the flu. I just met him in the washroom, and he says that he is very susceptible to colds. I remember once in Toungoo he was in bed with a cold. He is a very energetic person, and it riles him to have to be confined. "Joe" is taking care of him full time.

I certainly wish that I had brought my green Navy uniform and cap. Since we have no uniforms the fellows who brought their Army uniforms go around looking spic and span, and we who had been told not to bring them go around wearing our khakis. I need a pair of wool pants and the green trousers would be perfect. To have a pair made would cost about $800 or more. Woolen goods are extremely scarce here. One would think that this would not be true. That there would be many sheep here and places for manufacturing woolen goods. Instead the Chinese wear heavy layers of cotton cloth for the most part. Some of it is not very heavy, and I wonder how they don't freeze.

We have wonderful food served in excellent style for which we pay $1500 per month. Since I did not bring a pistol, I need one, and it would cost me several thousand dollars if I could find any for sale. The price of a package of chewing gum is $20 dollars. Some of the fellows have bought Army caps, which look like baseball caps and cost $70. I am going to get one tomorrow. A bicycle costs $3000, a gallon of gasoline $120. Today I sent a cable. Twenty five words cost $197.93, which is really very reasonable. A package of cigarettes costs $80, a haircut $4, this includes a shave and shampoo. A bar of soap costs $20, a pencil $10, a rickshaw ride of about 10 minutes $15, a handkerchief $45. Chinese money is in the same denomination as ours, and they have 1 cent, 5 cents, 10, 25, and 50 cents pieces like ours. As a matter of fact, I noticed that their paper money 1, 5, 10, 100 dollar bills are made by the American Banknote Company in New York. It takes some time to get accustomed to the idea of spending so many dollars for things that in the U.S. cost only a few cents. About the first thing I priced here was some woolen goods for making trousers. The cost was $480 per yard. At first this nearly takes your breath away. Yesterday I exchanged 100 rupees which I brought from Toungoo and received $1600 dollars. Boy, did I feel rich! That is until I began pricing things. The exchange rate in Burma when I left was about 3.29 rupees for one American dollar. The exchange rate here in Kunming yesterday was 16 dollars for one rupee. That makes 52 Chinese dollars for one American dollar.

Page 3 January 1, 1941

American goods are very expensive here. As I have said before, though local products are cheap their quality is so far inferior to anything made in the U.S. that they are only worth the little amount that they cost. Fortunately CAMCO brought much U.S. merchandise, and it is on sale in the canteen—otherwise things like Ivory or Camay soap, Colgate toothpaste, Carter's ink, razor blades, would be almost impossible to obtain.

We have been issued flight clothing, which is the same as that furnished to us in the Navy. They bought one quarter million dollars worth of it in the U.S. All the time it has been here in Kunming, and all the flying in Rangoon and Toungoo was done with ordinary sun-glasses and home-made helmets—or none at all—and khakis. Now we have two heavy jackets, fur lined gloves, pants, and boots. Three helmets, face mask, and goggles.

Here in Kunming we have excellent conditions, much better than in Toungoo. There are two bars, two recreation rooms, and baseball and volleyball diamonds. Yet a foreign country, though the Chinese have done their best to make us feel at home, is still so much different from being in the U.S. For example, the picture show in town that usually shows English-speaking pictures has a Chinese picture tonight. There is nothing to do outside of the hostel. I have associated with the other members of the group so much—living, working, and playing together all the time, that it would be nice to meet someone else or go out and get away for a few hours. In almost any large city in the U.S. there would be dozens of different things to do. One just has to get used to doing without many things that always before he has taken for granted. But I know this, that I will certainly know how to appreciate them if and when I return home. Yet someday after I have returned home and gotten used to those things again, the funny Chinese characters, Chinese music, the millions of Chinese that one sees on the roads, streets, and in the fields, the peculiar Chinese music, the feeling of being in a vast country old and historic with thousands of tales about its growth, will recur to my mind and I may want to return. However, right now my feeling is that I want to return to the good ole U.S. and live out my life in peace and rest.

Yesterday two former Army pilots who had contracts with CAMCO to be instructors here left to go back to the States. They received dishonorable discharges inasmuch as they quit when our Country was at war. If I had this letter finished they would have taken it back. As it is, I will have to wait until someone else goes back as this would never pass the censors.

This organization has made terrible mistakes that have cost it over a million dollars and other mistakes which have been irreparable. When you hear the reasons, of course, I could not have done better and few persons could. But I do want to discuss some of the mistakes. Chief mistake I consider to be the fact that they brought a large number of pilots who had never set foot inside a fighter or pursuit ship. Since I have been here I have about 15 hours in a P-40. None of this has been in gunnery. Consequently, I have not been in any engagement with the enemy. Prescott, Ricket, Rossi, Knapp, Keeton, Fish, Cavanaugh, Conant, Raines, Groh, and the fellow in Loi Wing are in the same boat. There are not enough planes to finish our training. We need combat, attack tactics, gunnery, altitude hops, in order to be ready. We could be ready in another 10 hours. This would give us about 25 hours in the P-40—we should have at least 50. In the U.S. Navy they wouldn't send up anyone in actual combat without much more than this. However, we will be ready to fight with another half dozen hours of gunnery and attack tactics. Now we have many more pilots than planes so we don't know when we will get more time. In the meantime our greatest good to the organization is that of reserve pilot material.

Now, if they had brought only experienced fighter pilots they would not have had to undergo the training that was given in Toungoo and consequently would not have lost 20 ships, which were washed out there. There were wrecked ships all over the place when we first got there. It was nothing to have two or three crashes a day. Every landing was a potential crash. Ricketts, who had had no previous fighter training, washed out three planes and one automobile. At least 20 other planes were damaged or washed out to what might have been accidents or inexperienced pilots. We had 100 planes. Now we have less than 50 which are in flying condition or which can be gotten into flying condition by such additions as new props or tires. Only three of these more than 50 planes were lost as a result of engagement with the enemy. This compares to our dead pilot list of six to date. Only two were lost as result of engagement with the enemy. I am not criticizing anyone. I am only pointing out facts. But like a Sunday morning quarterback, it's much easier to see later what could have been done earlier to prevent events from happening.

In the first place, Co. Chennault wanted only experienced fighter pilots. CAMCO started out trying to get them. They found that they couldn't get more than ten in both the Army and the Navy together. They also wanted pilots who were experienced in flying the P-40. This was harder yet. Finally they had to go down the line and get any pilot they could from the service. When I realized that in all of Pensacola they could only get 15–rather than 25 volunteers,

Page 4 missing

John's caption reads, "Training was expensive."
National Naval Aviation Museum collection

17. WE HAVE LOST AT LEAST SEVEN PLANES AND ONE PILOT

John writes the year 1941on this letter—the same mistake most people make the first few times in a new year. It's 1942, and as the war creeps closer it's becoming deadlier—costlier—in lives and equipment.

Praising Chennault, John writes he is "the guiding star that holds the organization together in a compact fighting unit."

In "Life" magazine, Bob Neale, 1st squadron armorer, also praised Chennault, saying, "The AVG went into battle with such eagerness because the 'Old Man' outlined a general plan and left details to the pilots. They knew everything there was to know about pursuits; he knew you were flying the ship and let you do it the way you thought best. That made for sunshine." Many referred to Chennault as "Old Man" because he was older than the rest of the AVG.

Jack Belden, author of the Life magazine article wrote, "This is no choral dance. This is a war. The A.V.G.'s and Chennault never cared for form or regulations and thought any method was correct that would ensure an operation striking at the right time with all available means. Paper-work was cut to a minimum. There was no waiting for O.K.'s from senior officers. Pilots did staff work. Brass hats in the Army poked fun at the lack of staff, but with what they had the A.V.G's did a hell of a good job."

John writes of fighting the Japanese Zero throughout his letters. They are more likely to have been the Nakajima Ki-43—the "Oscar." Or the Nakajima Ki-27—the "Nate." Both were slow, under-armed, and fragile—but highly maneuverable.

Occasionally, John refers to the planes as a ship—and refers to his blood chit as a "sign on our flying suits." The Flying Tigers were the first Americans to wear a blood chit. British pilots are credited with being the first blood chit carriers, but with a different name, the "goolie chit." The purpose was to communicate to friendly assistance in the local language in the event of their downed airplane. The blood chit is still used today by pilots in battle zones and has several languages of the region. The concept was good but there would be few, if any, combat pilots that admit it had ever helped them.

China is at once the richest and the poorest country on earth. Rich in that its natural resources have barely been tapped—poor in that its wealth per person is less than that of any other nation. Its 450,000,000 population is composed mostly of coolies and peasants. Agriculture is the chief enterprise. Most of the best cities of China have been taken by the Japs.

The country here is very mountainous, and flying over it is dangerous for this reason. It is easy to get lost because there are few landmarks like roads, railroads, dams, large factories, water tanks, power lines, and other distinguishable landmarks that make air navigation over most areas of the U.S. comparatively easy. The towns and villages look very much alike from the air, and there isn't much distinction between one mountain and another. Such things as radio ranges of course are out of the question. We have lost at least seven planes and one pilot because they have been unable to find our own or some other aerodrome upon getting lost. The maps of this country are very poor and then pursuit ships do not have a very large fuel capacity.

Because of censorship, I can't say much about our activities against the enemy except that which you have probably already heard or read about. In all we have shot down over 50 enemy aircraft with many other possibilities. Often enemy planes that are damaged will fall before reaching their own territory. Reports of these wrecks that are found come in sometimes days or weeks after the actual incident. Don't forget that most of this is wild and woolly country and transportation and communication are not what they are in the U.S.

I was in a poker game last night, and the average bets were $50 and $100 on each hand. I give my room boy $5 for picking up some film while downtown and donate $500 to the China Orphan Relief fund—all with complete abandon. In my pocketbook now is over $2500. Yep, I reckon I'm just another Croesus. I never fool with $1 bills anymore, and $5 and $10 bills hardly mean a thing to me. Really, I can't quite figure it out—especially in view of the fact that I only get $75 a month over here. Do you suppose that because it takes about 50 Chinese dollars to be equivalent to one U.S. dollar—that has anything to do with it? I wouldn't be surprised!

The Chinese dollar is theoretically stabilized at about 20-1 U.S. dollar. You can't buy any American money at 20-1, of course, because you could just turn right around and sell it for about 40-1. The Burma denomination similar to a dollar is the rupee. The exchange rate is 3.285 rupees for one U.S. dollar. The rupee market in Kunming fluctuates between 10-1 to 16-1 Chinese dollars for one rupee. The market now is about 15-1. Thus by getting U.S. money converted into rupees in Burma and then exchanged into Chinese dollars in Kunming we get the favorable rate of about 50 Chinese dollars for one U.S. dollar.

Despite this favorable exchange rate, prices of goods are still much higher than at home. This is due to the fact that China practically does no manufacturing at all at the present time. Even before the war she manufactured only about 10% of the goods she consumed–importing 90%. Now what imports there are, over her only source of supply–the Burma Road–are essential war needs. This means that a multitude of articles that we take for granted as available in almost any store in the States cannot be had for any price. Fortunately for us, there was a considerable quantity of toothpaste, soap, writing paper, toothbrushes, shaving cream, etc., sent over when the Group was first formed. These are available in the canteen at nominal cost.

The stores here are small shops, and the quality of the goods much inferior to what we are accustomed. Despite the cold weather here, woolen goods are scarcer than hens' teeth. It is difficult to imagine in what extreme poverty and hardship most Chinese live.

The few Chinese who are well off are terribly rich. The millions of Chinese who are poor, are dreadfully ill-housed, ill-fed, and ill-clothed. But with it all, the Chinese are a good-humored lot. Through thousands of years they have become accustomed to famines, floods, wars, and other hardships. To an American accustomed to steam-heated houses, smooth paved roads, ample sidewalks, large stores, convenient public transportation, clean stores with large choices of goods, newspapers, soda fountains, etc., a Chinese city like Kunming strikes one as being the most miserable place on earth. 99% of all commodities moved from place to place in the vicinity of Kunming are carried on the backs of coolies or donkeys. Sidewalks are so dirty, narrow, and crowded that a majority of persons have to walk in the streets. Until about four years ago there were no automobiles in this Province. Consequently most Chinese have not adapted themselves to the rapid motion of an automobile. They will begin to walk across the road directly in the path of a car travelling 30 or 40 miles an hour when it is hardly 100 feet away. When you barely escape running over a fellow by jamming on the brakes, he is bewildered at how the car came upon him so quickly. He is still adjusted to the relative speed of ox-carts, rickshaws, and his own method of transportation—walking. Consequently you can imagine the headaches one gets from driving through the crowded city of Kunming.

At the new aerodrome a new runway is being built. Several hundred women all day long take stones about the size of a watermelon or basketball and with a small iron mallet break this size stone into small bits. These small chips are then carried in baskets by coolies to the runway where they are poured out and smoothed over by hand. A large roller pulled by 50 or more coolies then presses the rock into a solid bed. The former jobs would in the U.S. be done by crushing machines and trucks and then later by steam rollers—with 1,000% more efficiency. But then, here in the East, time takes on a new aspect. There is not the rustle and bustle so characteristic of the Western world. Patience is these people's greatest virtue. It is nothing to haggle an hour over a single purchase.

But you should see the vegetables they grow here. These peasants would put American farmers to shame. They utilize every inch of the ground and produce the largest onions, turnips, carrots—the best-looking celery, cabbage, and kale that I have ever seen. They water the fields by carrying buckets of water from nearby ditches. We eat no raw vegetables, of course—boiling these as we do the water.

None of the buildings, including our own, have central heating systems or fire places. To heat our rooms round earthen pots, which burn charcoal, are moved in and out as needed. Most stores and shops have no heat at all. I have not seen a lump of honest coal since I have been here.

I understand that life in the States isn't quite what it used to be, what with increased taxes, decreased luxuries, and all-out production of war needs. However, there are probably none of us who would not like to be back there. The Group has been very successful thus far, however, and we feel that we can best serve our country, and China as well, by carrying on our jobs here. We are in particular need of more planes and parts, at present.

Nature has made this a beautiful country around here: huge mountains, large trees, green fields; combined with a cold climate at this time of the year which is either definitely invigorating or makes one want to curl up in a warm bed and sleep for a month.

I'm reading Gunther's "Inside Asia" again; this time, with more meaning. He certainly called the cards right on many of the events which have transpired since he wrote the book in '39. Also have read "Asia Odyssey" by Dmitri Alioshin and found out a lot about the Russian Revolution and how cruel men engaged in war can be—also, the hardships a human being can withstand and still live. We have a few such stories which have happened to members of the Group.

Marion Baugh, former Army flyer, on a flight to a nearby aerodrome in a North American trainer (NJ), crashed into the side of a mountain near Yunanyi. He was killed, and Terry, a radio man riding in the rear cockpit, was badly injured. After what is estimated to be a couple of hours Terry regained consciousness. There were a bunch of natives gathered about the wreck, but no one offered to extricate him. Both of his legs were broken, and he was pinned in badly as the ship was upside down. He couldn't talk Chinese, and they couldn't understand English. Finally he hit upon offering them money. Upon doing so they immediately set to get him out. Needless to say, it was a long time after before he reached a hospital and received medical attention.

Another pilot, Eriksen Shilling, former Army, had engine trouble and set his plane down on a mountain top about midway between Lashio and Kunming. The plane was completely wrecked, but fortunately Shilling was injured only slightly. The only thing he could do was stay with the plane and wait until someone arrived. That did not happen until the next day. As he did not have warm clothing with him, he nearly froze that night. He slept in his parachute, which he busted open and wrapped himself in. The next day some natives found him but were suspicious, despite the Chinese markings on the airplane. They would not let him leave nor did they offer him food or clothing. So another night was spent nearly freezing and also half starved. Finally, the next day some High Llama or elected official of some kind arrived and upon discovering who he was, they fed and clothed him warmly and hauled him in grand style 40 miles to the nearest road. Unfortunately, the other two pilots in the flight, Kenneth Merritt and Lacy Mangleburg—both former Army—got lost after Shilling went down and had to make crash landings. Both planes were demolished. Merritt escaped unhurt, but Mangleburg's plane caught on fire and he never got out. Then, just the day before yesterday, at Rangoon, Peter Wright—Class 132C, Pensacola—came in to land after being up on an air-raid alarm. Just as he was landing his Prestone—a pipe sprung a leak, and he couldn't see. His plane swerved off the runway and accidently crashed into a car in which Merritt was seated—killing him instantly. Paul Greene, former Army, bailed out over Rangoon when he was caught unaware by a dozen fighters, and his ship was shot to bits. Unfortunately, he opened his chute immediately, and a couple of fighters cut their throttles and glided down shooting at him all the while. Though they shot many a hole in his chute and creased him with several, he was not hit. But because his chute had so many holes in it, he descended very rapidly–hitting the ground with a bang, which knocked both his shoes off. After this incident, he was given a couple days leave to recuperate.

A few days ago, three A.V.G. and two R.A.F. fighters raided an enemy aerodrome in Thailand. They caught the Japs unaware and strafed planes on the ground, destroying seven or eight. Charles Mott, A.V.G.–former Army–crashed at low altitude as a result of machine gun fire from the ground. His plane was seen to burst into flames. If he is still alive, he is the only one of the Group to become a prisoner of war as yet.

Enough of these incidents. There are also others about George Paxton, Ed Overend, "Tex" Hurst, "Duke" Hedman, Tom Heywood, Parker Dupouy, and even John Donovan, and others. Some of these are incidents like when R.T. Smith surprised a Jap Zero fighter and let loose with all his guns and the Model "0" exploded–parts of the wreck damaging his own plane. Like when Dupouy cut off an enemy fighter's wing at the fuselage but managed to get back to our aerodrome with four feet of his own wing and half of his aileron missing. About how bullets creased the jaw–and the guys had burns to prove it–about how bullets came through the armor plated back of the seat but their velocity was so lost that they did not penetrate through the straps of the parachute. About how one day when we were up and Chauncey Laughlin was flying on me at the end of the echelon. He had engine trouble and had to make a crash-landing from which he walked away OK. But he was mad at me, when he finally got back to the field, for not having observed his trouble and following him down. How Ed Overend got a bullet in his controls, which made them practically useless, but how he managed to get the plane and himself down OK by landing in a rice paddy. Etc., etc., etc.

A few of us who have twin-engine experience may have the chance to fly with CNAC a couple of weeks and check out as co-pilots. You really have to hand it to the CNAC pilots. They bring a plane in, in any kind of weather. The worse the weather—the better they like it—because that means less chance of being attacked by Jap fighters. And they fly over some of the wildest country imaginable. We use CNAC often for transferring personnel and material back and forth.

The Burma Road is a remarkable bit of construction. But don't confuse it for a moment with Wilshire Boulevard in Los Angeles or the Outer Drive in Chicago. If you know of the roughest road in Alabama, then you have some idea of what it is like. After one trip, a truck is due for a major overhaul.

Three nights a week we have Chinese class taught by Peter Shih, graduate of George Peabody College in Nashville. He is the most enthusiastic Chinese, and one of the best professors I have ever met.

On the backs of our flying suits a sign is written in Chinese by the Generalissimo telling who we are and requesting whoever reads it to get in touch with our aerodrome—this is in case we have to land in the hinterland some place, and the natives won't mistake us for the enemy and shoot.

Without question, Col. Chennault is the guiding star that holds the organization together in a compact fighting unit. He has 100% support of everyone in the organization. We are a military organization, but the question of whether we are or not never arises. Everyone realizes that there is a real job to be done and that cooperation is essential if the group is to be successful. All of us feel that the Group is a successful fighting unit and has given good account of itself and will continue to do so. There is no such thing as saluting among members of the Group. The only one who holds any rank is the commanding officer, Co. Chennault. Strictly speaking we have no military discipline. What infraction of rules that occur are punished by fine–which money is turned over to the Group Revolving Fund. A pilot might go up and engage the enemy in a white shirt open at the collar, an old pair of cadet pants, and a Chinese Army cap. It has been found that the plane flies just as good, that the guns shoot just as straight, if not straighter, when the pilot is so dressed. Do not mistake me–no one dresses slovenly, but we feel that the matter of first importance is to defeat the enemy in every engagement, and this is always our first consideration. If a mechanic can work better with a long beard, or wearing tennis shoes, then he has the perfect right to do either or both. I am convinced that the organization is more efficient than if it were under Army or Navy jurisdiction. I have seen mechanics, armorers, radio men, work 10, 12, or 14 hours a day getting a couple ships in commission; proud that these ships were now ready to take on the Japs. Plane captains are just as proud of the number of enemy planes that their ship shoots down as the pilots. Pilots and men work together in close cooperation–both realizing that the services of each are indispensable.

In Rangoon we have been cooperating with the RAF. The general attitude of the Group is that the Limeys aren't doing all that they could. In the Xmas day fight at Rangoon we lost four planes and two pilots. The British losses were none–except planes on the ground. The pilots of RAF planes in the air said that we went in too close in our attacks on enemy bombers. We did go in close–but we shot down more than twice as many ships as they–plane for plane.

A characteristic of Americans seems to be to want to do better than the other fellow. An American achieves this by courageous assault, daring, and risk. The Britisher also wants to do better than the other fellow but not by risking so much. He would rather wait and be cautious. This is oftentimes a good policy, but in the case of war it can mean defeat in battle, as an enemy on the offensive wants just such a timid opponent.

We feel perhaps the British would not have lost those half-dozen or so planes on the ground if they had cooperated in being somewhat more aggressive.

On this particular Xmas raid, General Brett and Wavell landed on the airport not knowing that an air raid was in progress. As they stepped from their ship, a few bombs dropped on the field, and they dove into the nearest ditch, remaining there for over twenty minutes while the field was both bombed and strafed. It turned out later that they had come in for over 50 miles directly beneath the enemy formation without being seen.

It is almost impossible to see a plane that is camouflaged below you. When we take off and join up in formation the leader can rarely ever see the other planes coming up to join up on him. From below we can see the planes above us without too much difficulty. Our P-40's are so camouflaged that they blend in perfectly with fields, woods, and mountains, and not one time in a hundred would a plane above detect us if we are below.

Three days ago, three AVG and two RAF planes raided an enemy aerodrome in Thailand. They strafed Jap planes on the ground, destroying seven. One AVG plane burst into flames at a low altitude, as a result of machine gun fire from the ground, and crashed. If the pilot, Charles Mott, former Army, is still alive, he is the first of our bunch to become a prisoner-of-war.

Just now I learned that yesterday in Rangoon nine AVG P-40's and five RAF Brewsters raided another Jap aerodrome in Thailand and destroyed 24 planes on the ground, 3 trucks, and strafed enemy troops. All RAF and AVG planes returned.

Enough about war.

A college student at home–facing a post-war U.S. upon completion of his degree–would do himself well to learn Chinese and plan upon any of a thousand enterprises which are going to be open to American capital, industry, and science here in China when the war is over. As I see it, American industry is geared to such a high pitch now that when the war is over it will have to take it in its belt. Of course, there will be a market for automobiles and luxuries that are not being produced now, but with the great number of men released from the armed services there will probably be unemployment for a large number of workers. Then too, industry cannot cut production to one half or one third without causing a general depression. All this combined with the heavy tax bill that all citizens will have to share is going to make new markets, new opportunities for employment, necessary. With a backward country like China to develop, there need be no need of unemployment or lack of opportunity for American industrial and engineering skill and capital. China could utilize all the manufactured goods of the U.S., agricultural and manufacturing skill of American workers and engineers, and sanitation and hygiene knowledge of American doctors and scientists for the next 50 years. In turn, her natural resources have hardly been touched. No country is in a better position to benefit from the development of China–which is bound to come–than the U.S. This is due to the fact that China and the U.S. are very close and friendship between the two countries is rife. The impression that the AVG has made upon the Chinese has helped to bring about a welcome to other Americans.

美志願軍第一大隊
HEADQUARTERS
FIRST AMERICAN VOLUNTEER GROUP

IN REPLY REFER TO: John Donovan, P.O.Box 104, Kunming (Yunnan), China Jan.11, 1941

China is at once the richest and the poorest country on earth. Rich in that it's natural resources have barely been tapped - poor in that it's

John only used this official letterhead once. Correct date is January 11, 1942

"The Colonel"

John's caption

National Naval Aviation Museum collection

John's blood chit #247
National Naval Museum collection

John's caption reads "Steam Roller." National Naval Aviation Museum collection

18. LAST OF ALL, I WOULD NEVER FEAR DEATH

In this touching letter to his nephew Wayne Smith, the first son born to John's sister, Mary Ellen, he is frank, practical, and possibly foreseeing that he may not make it home. This is a true gift for Wayne—to be able to read the words of experience and wisdom from an uncle he never had the opportunity to know.

February 9, 1942
Kunming, China

Dear Wayne,

You are too young to know it now, but war is messy business. Someone beat me to it when they said, "War is hell."

However, there have always been wars and there will always be wars.

My idea is that a country should steer clear of wars if possible. The best way to do this is to be prepared to wage a war in order to enforce peace. By this, I mean that some countries will always be belligerent and aggressive. In order to preserve peace it will be necessary to wage war upon them before they strike our country first.

A good offense is the best defense.

If I were you, I would obtain a certain amount of military training, though this may be unpopular at the time, and you may never have the occasion to use it. I hope that in your generation there will be no wars.

Our country should keep abreast of the development of all military machines and tactics. In the previous World War, as in this war, we were unprepared. Being unprepared may someday lead to our defeat.

I believe in peace. I believe so strongly in peace that I think our country should pursue an aggressive peace policy. This can be best attained by a League of Nations or some similar organization, with police powers to preserve the peace. A League with full military powers to enforce its decisions is the only kind which will prove successful.

I do not believe in living by the sword nor am I a military man. However, I hope that I am realistic.

If I were you, I would obtain as much education as possible, but not any more than you are interested in obtaining. Education, as I mean it, includes travel, experiences, a realistic observation in people and things.

Instead of concentrating primarily on earning money, I would concentrate upon learning and developing as much as possible. Thus, money should come to you as a natural reward.

In your earlier years you will probably spend much thought in wondering what your place in society is to be, what life is all about, what other people think of you, etc. These answers will come to you only with the passing of the years. It is much more important that you live your life developing your general ability, so that you will be prepared to seize what opportunities may be open to you.

Above all you must feel that you are equal to other people. You must learn to feel this naturally. I say this in case you may have some tendency toward being shy, self-conscious, or sensitive. You must neither be arrogant or subservient. It is important that you develop a personality of your own.

If I were you, in my adolescent years, and afterward, I would manifest a frank, inquisitive attitude. You should never feel that because you are young there are many things you are not supposed to know. If I were you, I would be friends with everyone, younger and older people alike. I would never feel that there was a barrier between myself and anyone else. The richest boy or girl in town can be your best friend, likewise can be the poorest. Do not let the station of a friend's family interfere with your friendship. Remember that most of one's life is lived outside the family. Remember that when you are grown, your own station in life may be above that of the richest family in town. In the meantime, be a best friend to everyone.

As far as girls are concerned, have the same frank attitude toward them as toward anyone else. Feel that their friendship is just as desirable and never let there be a barrier between yourself and girls, as you should never let a barrier develop between yourself and any other person.

Last of all, I would never fear death.

Love and best wishes for a successful life,
Uncle John

19. THE BURMA ROAD CLUB

The air-raid alarm system throughout Free China (not occupied by Japan) was an enormous spider-net of people, radios, telegraph lines and telephones. It not only served to alert for enemy aircraft but also proved beneficial for lost friendly aircraft and locating downed pilots.

It seemed inevitable, almost everyone had done it—John damages his first airplane. Forced to abandon his plane, he had to get back to the base by truck. The only way to do this was to travel 200 miles up the Burma Road. Previously concerned he might leave China without having the opportunity to travel the famous route, John was pleased to announce he was a "full-fledged member of the International Burma Road Club."

John simplifies how important the Burma Road is calling it a "life-line."

March 5

Dear Folks,

We had a "jing baw" or air raid alarm a couple days ago. There was a report of some enemy planes down near the border. We took off but upon reaching our destination, found that the alarm was caused by some Chinese bombers flying in the vicinity. On our way back, our flight leader got lost. There was an overcast sky, and as I have said before there is nothing but mountains around here and most of them look just about alike. Fortunately, I had a fair idea of where we were and led the flight to a nearby airport. I was the first to land and ran into a small irrigation ditch, which was impossible to see until I was upon it. The plane jumped the ditch, but in doing so caused considerable damage to the plane. I crawled out of the plane and looked sickly at the first plane I had ever damaged. The other fellows of the flight benefited from my predicament and landed so as not to suffer the same fate. They later returned to Kunming. I was left to come back via convoy, which was then passing through this point.

The trip back over the Burma Road to Kunming took two days, by air the distance is 25 minutes. The trip by road is 340 kilometers. I could write a book on what I saw and experienced on this last lap of the Burma Road.

I was afraid that I would leave China without ever traveling the Burma Road. Now, I am a full-fledged member of the International Burma Road Club by reason of having traveled over 200 miles of this famous life-line.

Though the Japs know as much about this road as I, it is impossible to tell much about it because the British censors pass on all our letters, and they are very strict.

The best thing that I can say is that I wish everyone had the opportunity to travel over it. I really think it makes a change in a person. Seeing thousands upon thousands of coolies: men, women and children; working with their bare hands, breaking rocks into small bits like gravel, using nothing more than their hands—this does several things to a person. First it made me realize again how fortunate I was to be born in the U.S. Fortunate to be born of parents that could give me the opportunity to be educated and improve myself. Second, at the same time, it makes me feel so small. How insignificant was the puny amount of work that any one of these coolies could do. The vast amount of cutting through mountain sides, grading, clearing away landslides, carrying dirt and rocks on their backs for long distances to dump it on a section of the road that had washed out–all this done by thousands and thousands of workers–makes one realize how small the net contribution of any one worker–and at the same time, to one traveling over the road, it makes you realize how indeed small is the importance of one average person in the U.S.

Or elsewhere, and how puny his efforts and his accomplishment is considered–as the importance of one bricklayer to the building of the Empire State Building, one riveter to the building of a giant battleship. Third, it is a striking lesson in the old maxim that "An ounce of prevention is worth a pound of cure." I have my own object lesson in this, but to explain it would endanger this letter not passing the censors.

If one can imagine thousands upon thousands of coolies living beside the road from its beginning to its end, keeping it in repair, besieged by whirls of dust every time the thousands of trucks pass by; living in an area that was formerly uninhabited; breaking huge rocks with iron spikes–without the aid of one single piece of machinery, or cart, or truck, or wagon of any kind–doing this without knowing the why or wherefore of it all, then I say, that person has a much better imagination than I. Whereas I had flown over it many times, not before had I been down on the ground and saw what was actually going on. Anyone who has not been out of the U.S. cannot picture the living conditions, working conditions, and deprivations of these workers on the road, because there is nothing so crude in the U.S. to compare it.

I say that the Burma Road is a monumental piece of work considering what they had to work with.

Every pilot has been presented with a pair of Chinese wings, which we are proud of. We are, of course, members of the Chinese Air Force.

Will you let me know when you receive this letter and if any parts are censored? In sending letters here, I imagine the best way is to send them to:

John Donovan
c/o American Express
Calcutta, India
Thence Air Mail
Kunming
American Volunteer Group

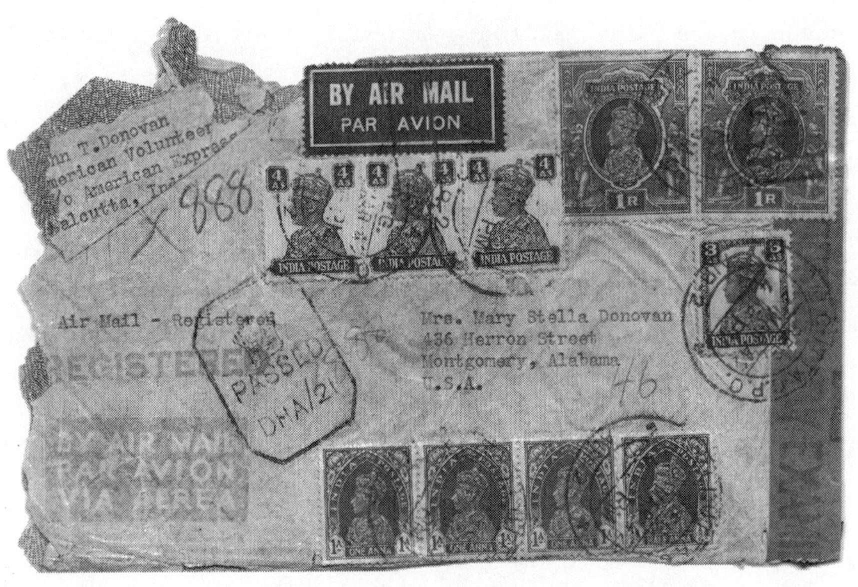

Photos courtesy of Kelleen Donovan Thornock

20. I WILL BE GLAD WHEN THIS IS ALL OVER

John is disheartened it has taken more than three months to receive the last letter from home. He is curious to know if and how much the censors cut from his last letter. It's now March, and he says the Christmas fruitcake still has not arrived. He reminds his mother to make sure all life insurance policies are kept current; he says he has not shot down too many "Japs" but is doing his part. With many questions about family members, he yearns to stay connected with what is going on at home and continues to share his life with them. For the first time he requests items he wishes he had brought with him.

March 7, 1942

Dearest Mother and folks,

By now I bet Wayne weighs 50 lbs. If so, he should be carrying his mother around and not vice-versa. A week or so ago I received the very nice picture of him, which Sis sent together with Xmas cards. I have not received the fruitcake, which Mother sent.

The most recent letter from home that I have received was

mailed Nov. 10. It was delivered to me about Feb. 27. How many letters from me have reached home? Were any censored? Will you let me know when you receive this letter?

Business matters: the check from CAMCO for Sept. salary $445 was correct inasmuch as my pay with them did not start until Sept. 5. All subsequent deposits should be for $525. I may have my salary out here increased to $100, which will make my deposit at home $500.

You should keep both my insurance policies, but CAMCO should pay the premiums. If they do not, then you should see that they are paid or pay them. The money for the payment of the premiums on my insurance is supposed to be deducted out of the portion of my salary, which I receive over here. I hope that you have the matter of my insurance taken care of so that both the Union Ministers and Veterans policies are kept in force all the time.

Will you write the McDonald Oil Company on Barrancas Avenue, P.O. Box 1122, Pensacola, Fla., and ask them what the balance of my bill with them is? I think I owe them $32.86. If this is correct, then please mail them a check.

Have you heard from my claim for payment of $400 bonus for 11 months' service in the Navy? If not, then let's forget about this matter.

How are cousin Alvin and Army flying getting along? How do Sis and Paul like country life? They should be getting rich if farm products are as high as we have heard rumors that other commodities have become. There is money to be made during war times and knowing Paul for a shrewd businessman, he is no doubt making his share. Received a letter from James mailed Nov. 14. I understand that since then he has gone to Washington to work. If any place is a humming buzzing metropolis, Washington should be the place. I hope that he is still there and doing well. I hear infrequently from Mary

Jane and Sybil. Mary Jane has been the best friend of all. I have received more letters from her than anyone. In total, Mother has written as much as Jane, I should say. The most recent letter from the States was from Roy and Clara Davis and was mailed December 5. Thus, you can easily see that when letters do arrive, there is a mad scramble with everyone trying to find one for himself.

Instead of bringing as little as possible with me, I realize now that I should have brought as much as possible, for over here one can sell anything at three or more times what it costs in the U.S. Will you check upon sending me a few things like a radio, camera, sun-glasses, top-coat, pistol, and ammunition, etc.? Inquire whether such articles are allowed, if they can be insured, tariff rates, etc. Packages for AVG members are not charged the usual import duty into China. I could use these articles and when I leave could sell them. You can get an idea of what they are worth here when I say that I sold my blue Navy overcoat for $150 American. Do not send anything unless you are guaranteed that it will reach Calcutta, c/o, AVG, or, not reaching there, the value of the contents will be reimbursed.

I am in good health and getting along fine. To date, have not shot down too many Jap planes, but am doing my share. Naturally, I will be glad when this is all over, and I get back home. However, in the meantime, I am not too unhappy—except on occasion.

Whereas the small sum we have in the bank would be a tidy sum five or six years ago, now with inflation and high prices it is a mere pittance. You can do with it as you wish. I would think that the best thing would be to try to make this sum worth something like what it would be worth in ordinary times by using it in a manner to increase it. However, you do with it as you will and use it as if it were yours alone.

Love and best wishes to all,
John, Jr.

P.S. Concerning sending packages—maybe the Pan American Ferry Command will bring packages for AVG. If so send my green Navy uniform, amber-colored lenses for goggles, good wrist watch, fountain pen, and movie camera with plenty of Kodachrome film. Any of these things I can use up to $500.00 worth.

John Tyler Donovan 3rd Pursuit Squadron
Hell's Angels
National Naval Aviation Museum collection

FEBRUARY AND MARCH NEWSPAPER ARTICLES

Morning, March 25, 1942 — 10 Pages — Price 5 Cents

40 Jap Planes Destroyed In U. S. Volunteers' Raid

Surprise Attack On Thailand Airport Baffles Foe

Tokyo Uneasy

Hiraide Warns Its Public To Expect Hard Fight

Burma Forces In Maneuver For Offensive

Chungking Army Eager To Face Invader; U. S. Fliers Spread Havoc

Burma Forces In Maneuver For Offensive

Churchill Confident

James Donovan's personal collection of newspaper articles. He saved every article he found that mentioned John or the Flying Tigers.

21. I HOPE THIS LETTER REACHES HOME

April was the turning point for the AVG. Their equipment was deteriorating, casualties were mounting, and they were outnumbered in every battle. Chennault knew they could not continue this way for long. There was pressure from Washington to send in an American military unit. The discussion to disband the AVG took hold, and it was decided the AVG would conclude its mission in July; those who wanted to stay could, and those who chose to leave could do so.

Even with plans to disband in two months, the Group remained ready to fly into battle every day.

Conversely, Chennault was also under pressure from China to use his influence to persuade the Group to remain. In Russell Whelan's book, "The Flying Tigers," he quotes Chennault, "They deserve to go home if they want to. Much as I regret their disbandment, I know they can just stand so much." And, as always, Chennault praised his men: "They were the finest bunch of fighting fliers the world ever saw. I owe much to them because they gave me the greatest opportunity any air force commander ever had—to train and direct, in complete freedom of action, a group of brave and skillful military aviators."

Also, in April, Chennault was recruited by Washington and promoted to Brigadier General while still commanding the AVG. Preparation began for the transition to the China Air Task Force which Chennault would command in July when the AVG disbanded.

In this lengthy, multiple-day letter, John describes meeting the Generalissimo and Madame after attending a banquet honoring the AVG.

He admits to being lonesome and homesick but doesn't dwell on it.

As for the AVG transition, John says the Navy and Army would never fly the AVG planes because of the shabby condition they're in. Regardless, John and the Group are proud of their accomplishments against the Japanese and still wish they had more planes.

April 2, 1942
First American Volunteer Group
P.O. Box 104
Kunming, Yunnan, China

I admit to being lonesome and homesick. What a joy it would be to drive a car down a smooth American boulevard with modern stores and homes on both sides! This, instead of riding in a rickshaw pulled by a coolie down a bumpy cobblestone narrow street with rickety stones and houses on each side–dirt and filth everywhere.

However, the Chinese treat us like kings. Our living quarters are comfortable and clean, the food is good, and we live better than 90% of the population. Still, as I have said before, one cannot maintain an American standard of living here–at any cost.

It is difficult for one who has not visited a foreign country like this part of China to realize the many things one has to do without when living here. The thousands of articles in any department store at home would bring good fortune if moved in total to Kunming. The merchandise in any department store in the States are almost priceless luxuries here. With all of China's sea coast taken, the supplies that come in are principally of a military nature.

When this war is over it will be fun to visit some of the better Chinese cities like Shanghai, Peking, Canton, Nanking, etc.

Kunming is a "boom" town and probably the most prosperous in all China at the present. It is a relatively new city, which has become accustomed to automobiles within the past five years. The town itself has been here a long time, but its position on the Burma Road has brought it a new importance.

When flying over this country, the most noticeable things of all are the mountains, which reach to a much greater height than the altitude of the city itself, which is about 6000 feet. From the air the old wall, which encircles most of the city, is clearly visible. When flying low enough, one can see into the courtyards of the old type of Chinese homes. Fields of rice and vegetables cover the entire landscape. Even the sides and tops of mountains are cultivated and irrigated. Sampans spot the surface of the lake, and when there has been no encounter with the enemy recently and we crave a little excitement, it is fun to dive lower over a sampan and pull up suddenly so that slip stream from the propeller hits the sails and sends the boat scurrying across the water.

Yesterday, I received the December 15 issue of Time. Perhaps this is the latest copy in all of China. I am sure that it is the only magazine received by any member of the Group from the U.S. since the war began. It was read with avid curiosity by all. I have always enjoyed reading Time and have high regard for its clear-cut, concise, though sometimes inaccurate, news. I hope that Mother will have the mailing address changed to Box 104, Kunming.

The Group feels proud of its accomplishments against the

Japanese. With more planes we could destroy all of the enemy air force that we could contact. As it is, we have had to operate with the smallest number of airplanes imaginable. We have flown planes that would have been condemned by the Army or Navy at home. However, we feel that we have made a good record considering that we have been far outnumbered in every engagement with the enemy thus far. Sometimes we ponder what immense damage we could inflict upon the Japs if we had just one U.S. day's production of P-38s, P-39s, P-40s, and B-17s.

I hope this letter reaches home. It is discouraging to have written often and not have the letters get through. I gather that they have not from cablegrams I have received. Mail from here now goes to Calcutta via CNAC where it is censored and then to the U.S. c/o American Express.

The fellows who drove trucks or cars from Burma to Kunming have formed a "Burma Road Club." They have hair-raising tales of narrow escapes, of seeing numberless trucks which had rolled over embankments and smashed to bits before hitting the bottom of deep gullies, of going around narrow curves on the side of the mountain where, if they had encountered another truck, they themselves might have gone over the cliff. Few of them would make the trip again for as much as a thousand dollars, but none would take a thousand dollars for their experiences. Like most of the other pilots, the Burma Road to me is a narrow winding strip, which goes up, down, and around mountains, over rivers and ravines, and is sometimes completely hid from the view by clouds.

Tonight the entire personnel of the Group are to be the guests at a banquet to be given by the Generalissimo and the Madame. Today I saw both of them for the first time. To me he looked older, thinner, and more worried than I had imagined him to be. She is vivacious, attractive, energetic, with a much more striking personality than most women possess.

I have now returned from the banquet, which I enjoyed much more than most banquets. I must revise my description of the Generalissimo. When I saw him for the first time this morning he was preparing to address the senior members of his staff in this area, including the Governor of this province, General Yuen. Tonight, he was much happier, as he knew that he was among friends, none of whom were questioning his conduct of the war, and he was not questioning our activities against the enemy. He was well pleased with our record, he said, and considered us as his own officers and men. I must say that tonight he looked not so old, nor so thin, nor so worried.

Concerning the Madame, I can only enlarge on what I have already written. She is well-preserved for her age and has a perfect figure. She absolutely captured our hearts. Col. Chennault has always adored her, and now she has the adoration of every member of the AVG. She has a superb sense of humor and is a good sport. One might think she could be a little wicked. She admitted to being interesting. When she rose to speak, her first words bespoke an intellectual. She gathered the entire group up into her arms and called us "her boys." This, despite the fact that she doesn't look a day over 28. Her eyes are the most noticeable thing about her. She was a much better speaker than most and a much better man than many. She was at once a mother, an attractive bewitching girl, a counselor, a wit, and a sternly disciplined person who encouraged us to discipline ourselves. She was as much at home speaking before the entire group as if she had been talking to one person. We cheered her to the rafters time and again. She earned the respect and admiration of all. She is definitely a superior person and the Generalissimo would be lost without her. Both are idealists but factual.

Fortunately I had a seat not five feet from both. At all the other nearby tables were other pilots. As I looked from one to the other, I knew at least one story about each. Some were good for several stories. The Generalissimo was worth several that I knew of. A good story about the Madame was her part in the Sian kidnapping, when she with the help of Donald, secured Chiang's release. None of the stories were told at the banquet, of course, but some of them occurred to me, as I sat there reflecting just what kind of people these were.

The pilot on my right had a black eye resulting from a recent parachute jump when his plane was shot up. The one on my left had crashed into a Jap plane in the air and flown back over 100 miles to our field with half of his right wing torn off. The eyes of the fellow across from me were still irritated from particles of glass which had gotten into his eyes when a bullet burst through the canopy of his plane and passed a couple inches from his head, while in combat. Next to him was a pilot who had been forced down in enemy territory but had found a friendly native who took him through Jap lines to safety. Another had a Jap plane shoot off his tail by two pilots but didn't know that the Jap was behind him shooting at him until he got back to the aerodrome. Another was surprised by Jap planes, which dove at him from out of the sun, and he still has some lead in his back which broke through a joint in the armor plate. Another was up on an engineering hop, without an oxygen mask, and seeing an enemy observation plane, managed to get up to 16,000 feet without undue comfort and shot it down. So on and so on, the stories are numberless, and they are being added to every day.

Goodness, but I have felt old lately. I don't like this. I have felt like 45. I have always vowed that if I have any children I would remain agile, playful, and energetic—no matter what my age—so that I could play games and be on good terms with them. The way I have felt lately, however,

I would be an old sourpuss if I were a father. War, of course, is a grim business, but there is no need of becoming a loggerhead. I attribute part of this feeling of "oldness" to lack of fresh fruit and vegetables in our diet, together with a lack of milk. Since leaving the U.S., we haven't had a taste of sweet milk or buttermilk. Neither do we have here in Kunming any fruit juices of any kind. Coffee, tea, and water are the drinks served at every meal. Part is due to lack of recreational opportunities. If we were in an American city there would be many people that we could associate with who would not actually be engaged in fighting the war. As it is, we live and work together continually as a Group, consequently fighting the war is the principle subject on everyone's mind.

Today is the day after the day of the banquet. Yesterday five of us together with an interpreter rented a sampan and went duck hunting. I wish everyone I know could have made the trip. Propulsion of the sampan was made by means of three huge cars, which were leashed to gun-whales by rawhide strips, instead of operating in car locks, which would be too expensive for the owner to purchase. In the stern position was the owner, a Chinaman about 40 with a most cheerful expression. His daughter, about 10 years old, operated the center car and worked like a Trojan throughout the trip. The wife and mother worked at the car and bow. The five of us felt somewhat squeamish when we got out into the lake and the going got tough as we were heading to windward. The three oarsmen had to lean to with a will to make a way at all. I tried to get the little girl to let me lend a hand. The only ones not uncomfortable that the girl and woman should be working so hard while we sat back and enjoyed ourselves were the four Chinese on board. The Chinese interpreter did not approve of my offering to help since the girl, mother and father, the Chinese interpreter, myself, and everyone else on board would lose "face."

The sampans are not painted and seem to be caulked with concrete. Some families live aboard these boats year in and year out. Some drawn up to the bank were busy cooking, eating, or washing clothes. On each side of the canal at intervals are mud huts in which farmers lived that tilled the fields that were irrigated by ditches leading out from the canals.

There were many ducks in the canal and in the fields and ponds on each side of the canal. These were domestic ducks, however, and they keep together in droves. Since they are not penned in and have free rein to go where they please, it is a mystery to me how the farmer keeps from losing them. Some duck hunting parties have fired at these domesticated ducks with the result that the owner comes out waving, shouting, and otherwise making known their disapproval.

A couple miles down the canal we found a park, which we had not seen before. Walking through it we saw many flowers of different colors, which resembled azaleas. There were also temples, peacocks, a bear, and a couple deer. Many Chinese were rowing about in the lake there, and it was easy to see that Spring was in the air as most of these small row boats contained a girl and a boy dressed in their Sunday best. Though this place was by no means a Westlake Park as Los Angeles boasts, it was something on the idea.

Whereas we were all eyes observing new sights and watching the people that were all about, wherever we went we always drew a crowd that was bent upon watching us. This is very amusing. If we are downtown making a few purchases a crowd invariably collects to watch. Usually we drive out to any numerous lakes that are around Kunming when we wish to hunt ducks. This place abounds in ducks. I shoot them with an automatic 22 rifle. Some of the fellows have shotguns but most of us use rifles. A few even shot at ducks with pistols. No matter where we are hunting, after we have fired a few shots a crowd gathers around us and before we leave sometimes there are as many as several hundred Chinese about. One of the reasons for their pursuing us is to pick up the empty brass shells. For these they will go out into the water to retrieve ducks that have fallen there. A few days ago one of the pilots had a forced landing about 40 miles from Kunming in an area where one would think not a person lived for miles. We located him about an hour later, and when I flew over the place it was swarming with a crowd of Chinese that I would estimate to be at least 5,000 in number. Verily. They seem to come out of the ground.

After shooting for a while in the lake, we notice a nearby island that seemed to be the home of a wealthy family. It turned out to be the residence of the head man of the municipality of Kunming. We asked the guard for permission to walk through the courtyards and inside we found so much more of the azalea-looking flowers, hollyhocks, water lilies, ferns, etc. The furniture in the rooms into which we peered was modernistic. There was a glass-enclosed study in one of the courts which gave me an idea for the same.

From this spot we went to a small island on which there were many grouped mud huts. We prowled around looking in some of the residences and found that the stables and the homes were the same. Also, we found a couple of gambling games in progress which broke up as we approached. No amount of encouragement would make them continue. At these games were children, women, and men. A gambling game always interests me, and I would have liked to watch them. These people are shy at having their picture taken. Since they would not pose we had to catch them unaware.

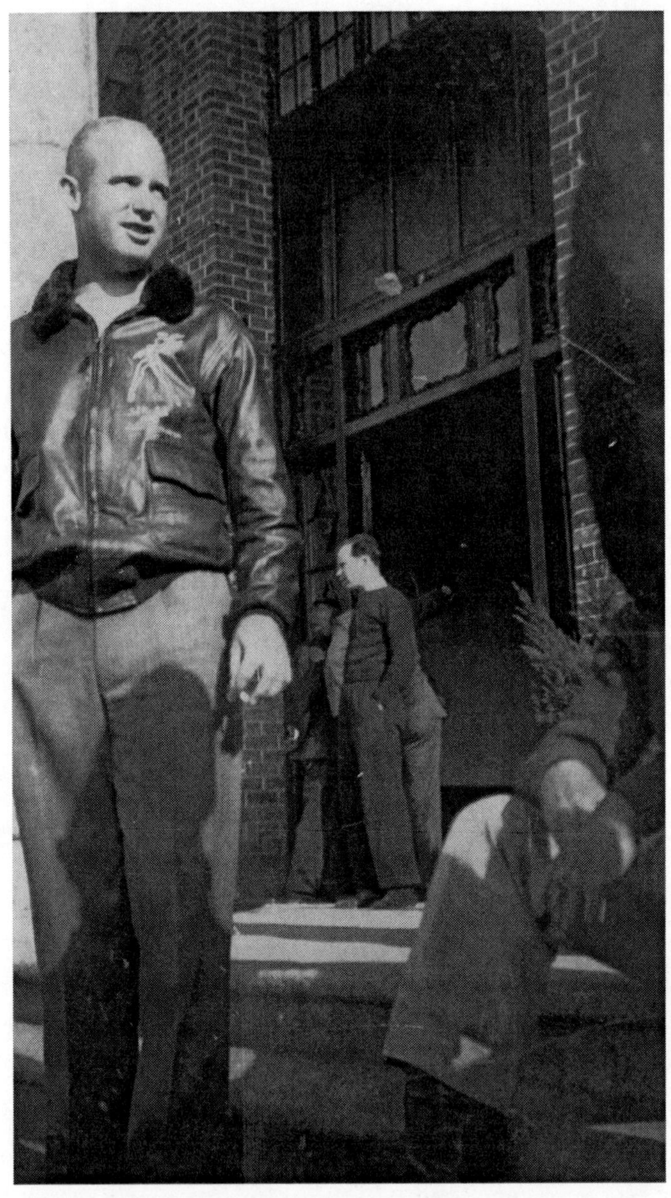

"Awaiting Chiang Kai-shek" John's Caption
National Naval Aviation Museum collection

22. BIG RED CIRCLE

This is the only letter to Jane, John's high school friend, in the preserved collection of letters at the National Naval Aviation Museum in Pensacola, Florida. Like family friend Sybil, Stella and Jane often shared the communication they received from John.

Life is not the same back in Montgomery since the war began. Or anywhere in the United States that matter. Tires and cars are the first two items to go on a ration list. Gasoline was added to the growing list of commodities. Production dramatically declined on everyday items when the manufacture of war items skyrocketed.

John asks Jane to share this particular letter with his mother because he had "talked shop" too much and didn't know when he would have a chance to write again.

The first U.S. troops arrive in Australia in April 1942. The Australians had thought the British would come to their aid but Winston Churchill made it clear they needed all their resources to remain in their own country to defend itself.

On the Bataan Peninsula of the Philippines, U.S. and Filipino troops were low on food and ammunition and had no choice but to surrender. Japanese troops forced about 76,000 prisoners to march 60 miles in the blazing tropical sun. This is well known in the history of the war as the Bataan Death March. At least 5,200 Americans died on the march. Decapitation, bayonetting, and sitting for hours in the hot sun without water are only a few of the documented atrocities.

Sixteen U.S. bombers, led by Lt. Col. James Doolittle, took off from an aircraft carrier, the USS Hornet, 800 miles off Tokyo and made the first bombing raid against Japan on Japanese soil. It was a real American morale booster to finally avenge the bombing of Pearl Harbor.

In the United States, an immense fear of spies on American soil caused the government to isolate over 100,000 Japanese-Americans in "relocation" camps in isolated areas. They were free to leave January 1945, following the end of the war.

Monday after Easter Letter
Number 5 April 6, 1942

Dear Jane,

Received your number 1 letter of the year three days ago. This is at least the 5th letter to you this year–as I have numbered it according to your suggestion.

Gal, I sho' enjoy receiving letters from you. Always have. Then, you have always known how much a guy appreciates letters when at camp as a result of several brothers who went to camp, but more likely it wasn't you. You probably used to get letters yourself when you were at camp.

I hope that I never forget how much camping used to mean to me–because if I ever have a boy or a girl of camping age, and they begin to act crazy about camping–I will understand, even though it will mean their being away from home. But, then if I'm not a successful parent, I'll be glad to get rid of them, and they'll be glad to get away from home. That would in my estimation make a complete failure out of any otherwise successful person–i.e. to be a failure as a parent. Since I don't anticipate giving birth to any children soon, I'll go on to other subjects.

If you did the printing on the envelope of this last letter (and I think you did, though I've never seen much of your printing), I must say it is very good.

This is written as I sit in "my" truck (which is part of my equipment as mess officer—this job in addition to my duties as pilot). I look up and see the P-40s on the runway. The alert shack is about 50 feet away. In it, on days when we are "alert," we play acey-deucey, read, play ping pong or cards—or sleep. As the weather is adverse today, I don't think there will be any activity against the Japs, so this is a good time to write you.

We are right on the Burma Border—where China meets Burma. That's the name of a book I have been reading. It was written by Beatrix Metford. After reading most of it, I wondered what she looked like. Thumbing through the book the only thing I could find was a picture of her riding in a sedan chair. This showed her legs. That much of her was quite interesting.

If I ever see a white woman again, I know she'll look so pale that I'll surely think she is sick.

Bamboo poles grow around this place in profusion. Our alert shack, as are most of the other buildings and homes, are made of nothing but bamboo. The bark or shavings or leaves from the bamboo is used to make the hatched roof. The poles are used for the framework and the poles split and pressed flat are used for weaving the sides. A house built in this manner, without a nail or solid board, is rain proof, cool, and fairly long lasting. As I look around in a 360° circle the entire 10 or 12 houses and buildings that I see are all built of bamboo. So you see how easy it is to build yourself a house. I really think you would like such a house. Table, chairs, beds can be made of bamboo. Such a house would be swell near the beach or in the mountains in summer. But then at home we could not get such bamboo. This bamboo looks like cane used for fishing poles at home. The main difference being that the bamboo here rises to a height of over 100 feet and is often more than 6 inches in diameter.

Today is Thursday–three days after the preceding two pages were written. I forget what interrupted this letter, but I think it was a volleyball game. I'm quite sure that was the attraction. We played until time to go back to the barracks, which are about 13 kilometers away. The following day I was off duty. Between "jing baws" or air raid alarms, I was busy taking care of the many things that are needed for the comfort and convenience of the pilots and men here–matters of importance ranging from door springs, mosquito netting, firewood for stoves and hot water heater, to the safe-keeping of the thousands of rupees needed with which to purchase supplies. That night we had our first movie here. "Here Comes the Navy" (about a 1934 production, I think) some of us have been wondering where the Navy was, so we were glad to see it on the screen.

The next day, Wednesday, was yesterday. I was on duty or "alert" as we say. As usual we had an alarm about 8:30. We went up, but it was only a Jap 2-engine bomber observation ship. Two guys took out after it but using all the manifold pressure they could get–they could not gain on it. The guy closest to it shot one down the day before just like it–but then he had an altitude advantage. What with twin row Pratt and Whitney engines, these Jap ships get up a lot of speed. We stayed up patrolling about an hour and went down over Lashio, but no more Japs came around.

I probably shouldn't be telling you this, but in your letter you said I never talk "shop"–so I think I'll talk a little "shop."

As we were eating lunch, which is brought out to us at the alert shack by Chinese boys, the telephone rang, and there was a report of an unidentified aircraft headed our way. So we rushed to our ships again and are in the air within a few minutes. This rushing to your ship and getting in the air is not at all uncommon, but more often than not it is a false alarm.

Three of us flying together and we are headed south to intercept the enemy plane and still climbing at 23,000 feet. My radio is out so I don't know what the score is when the other wing man begins rocking his wings violently, dipping them, pointing back toward the field. I figure he is having engine trouble and say to myself, "Why in the hell doesn't he go back without trying to take us with him?" But then the leader starts diving down towards the field, and I think then that this was just another false alarm. We are a couple thousand feet and right above the field when a couple planes turn toward me and started shooting.

Right then I realized how careless I had become. I had been fighting in this war just long enough to become indifferent and careless—instead of "staying on the ball" as one has to at all times.

Well, I had been shot at before, but never had I been more scared. Here I am, kinda disgusted at what I thought was another false alarm and just getting ready to prepare to land. It was the sudden realization of my own stupidity that made me so scared. Here I am with a bunch of Jap fighters literally all around me—and I had been as unsuspecting as a baby. I felt more helpless than a baby and wouldn't have bet ten cents on my chance of getting out.

The other two guys were aware because their radio was working. They began tangling with the Model Zero, which is considered to be the best Jap fighter. Fortunately the other wing man shot a Model Zero right off my tail. I then began to turn with another, but he made me look silly as they can turn inside a P-40 any day. Fortunately, there was a small cloud at about 3000 feet, which was nearby. I headed for it. Japs won't fly in a cloud if they can keep out of them. I was thoroughly frightened, and I needed a moment to "wake up." In the cloud I flew round and round for a moment and came out full of wim, wigor and witality. Right away I saw a "dead chicken." By that I mean I say a Jap what was "cold turkey." Need I explain that? He had just dove on the field, strafing a Blenheim bomber which the damn British had there, and was pulling up. I came in from the rear quarter and let loose a burst and immediately he caught fire and drove straight down into the ground. I don't like that low altitude fighting. Right away I was in a mess again as another Zero was turning toward me just when I was about to shoot another one. I shot a short burst but missed and dove down and skipped along the trees to get away. I turned to see if I was followed. Since I was not, I came back, got in a few shots at a couple more, and then saw one that I felt I could get. I shot a short burst at him and smoke began pouring from his motor. Then my attention was diverted trying to get away from another one of those devils.

After getting away, I headed South thinking that I could get at them again as they headed for home. I climbed up thinking that surely this was just a prelude to a good juicy bombing.

After waiting about 35 minutes and not seeing anything, I came back to the field and landed. The other wing man, that I mentioned before, said that he saw me shoot at this Jap that began to stream black smoke like a choo-choo train, but the Jap did not go down—so he finished him off. Since we only get credit for planes that actually crash immediately, disintegrate in the air, or catch on fire (and smoke coming from the plane doesn't count), I got only one in that fight.

If I had been on my toes, and if my radio had been working, I could have gotten at least three.

In all we shot down 10 for sure with 2 probables. Men on the ground counted 13 Japs in all. Not many got home. There was not one hole in one ship in the air. The only damage they did was to shoot up the Blenheim and (God knows how we hated this) burned one and completely riddled another brand new P-40, (Kittyhawks) which had been brought in the day before by Pan American pilots. To have to lose these two planes on the ground when we need planes so bad was a real tragedy.

Apparently the Japs can afford to lose 10 out of 13 planes, because they always come back with a flock of new planes the next time.

Three model Zeros crashed right near the edge of the field. They apparently dove straight in for the motors and pilots were buried and parts of the fuselage are scattered over a hundred yard area. I have pictures of the wrecks. One of the men has a good movie camera and could have taken some magnificent movies but he was out of film.

Today I was off duty again. As I say, we have twice as many pilots as planes. Most of the day was spent driving my truck around hauling supplies, cots, etc., back and forth. We had two air raid alarms today, and I spent part of the time on a nearby hill thinking maybe I might see some action from the ground—but nothing happened.

I am on duty again tomorrow. You can depend that they'll be here again. And we used to think they didn't have many planes and what they did have were no good. You should see these slick jobs they fly. Self-sealing gas tanks, maneuverable as a training plane, fast as a P-40, 10 mm. machine-guns, retractable landing gear, low wing monoplanes.

And does that red circle on their wings look "big" when they surprise you.

I enjoy this Mess Officer job that I have. It keeps me busy. I have charge of a bunch of coolies, house boys, #1 boys, cooks, etc. They work hard to please the pilots and men. Naturally even a squadron clerk is a hero to the Chinese. The few Indians and Burmese employed say, "Yes, Mawster"–"Coming, Sahib."

I wouldn't want to live with me when I get back to the States. I would be doing something when I needed a little assistance and would probably yell out "H-E-Y B-O-Y!" and would be expecting to hear "Yes sir, coming" (Chinese boy) or "Coming, Sahib," Indian boy. "Coming, Mawster" Burmese boy. Whether they are 10 or 90 you call them boy anyway.

It's getting to be midnight, and I have to be "alert" at 5:30 so I better hit the hay. I will give this letter to the Pan American who is leaving tomorrow. I would like to know if and when you get this letter. Also if you have received any of my other letters written this year. Will you let Mother read this or have the parts which she may be interested in since I may not have another opportunity soon to get a letter out. I started out to write you strictly a personal letter and now I have to ask you to share it. I was going to write another to Mother, but I started talking "shop" and used up all the time so that now I have only this letter ready, and he is leaving tomorrow morning. Maybe he can put this on Ferry Command at Cairo and get it back that way. I hope so.

Thanks again and I sure did appreciate your letter. Please drop by to see Mother again if you have the chance.

I hope James is in a defense job instead of the Army. One guy out of a family in the fight is enough. Consider how badly we need airplanes. Especially airplanes that are faster, have more armament and armor plating, climb to a higher altitude, have better radios, more visibility, etc., etc.

Glad to hear about the negative examinations and you will be more careful about your work. When I say will—I mean you must. Glad that you enjoyed your few days after Xmas stay in Montgomery. Sorry to hear about Bill Dubois. Will you give him my best regards when next you see him? I always liked him. Also, George Gill—he appealed to me, too. I'll never forget him. (Hey I'm talking as if he were a girl.) Glad your Mother is looking better—that must mean that she's a beauty indeed—because she always looked good to me. I am looking forward again to seeing her. Tell her I'm bringing something from China with me for her. But only if she's got some of that good wine that I like.

You must not work too hard and if the PhD isn't forthcoming this year—well, all right! If I had a few thousand idle dollars I would trust Noble to have it and make more with it. His building Negro houses is a good idea. If he had built them two or three years ago—a still better idea!

How is the niece or nephew? Is he or she taking good care of the parents? How are your flag lilies, daffodils, and narcissus? Of these three, I like the daffodils most. Narcissus is pretty, too, and oh, so good smelling. Get some cape jasmine and put it near William's nose when he's sleeping and see if he doesn't say that he had pleasant dreams!

Love,
John

John's caption : "House boys" with John.
National Naval Aviation Museum collection

John's caption: "Sometimes it was."
National Naval Aviation Museum collection

APRIL 10, 1942 ASSOCIATED PRESS ARTICLE "FLYING TIGERS TOO MUCH FOR JAPS (AP)

ENEMY'S FINEST AIRCRAFT EASY; MONTGOMERY MAN IN THICK OF FIGHTING

(Though the following dispatch from Daniel Deluce has been 14 days in transit from the remote interior of embattled Burma, it remains a graphic picture of the grim battle against great odds being fought by the heroic "Flying Tigers" of The American Volunteer Group. Thursday, according to the latest battlefront communiques, the boys of the AVG still are waging that fight, in the face of the constantly rising Japanese strength.)

BY DANIEL DELUCE

WITH THE AMERICAN VOLUNTEER GROUP IN BURMA APRIL 10, 1942–delayed–(AP)

Driven out of Mingaladon and then Magwe, the fighting Yanks of the American Volunteer Group, with the colors of China and Britain on the plane wings, now are braced against the inevitable heavy Japanese assaults on their new base defending North Burma.

Already they have cracked down on the enemy's numerically superior forces and have destroyed an entire squadron of the invader's finest aircraft.

In two dogfights spaced 48 hours apart, ranging 100 miles over the green mountains of China's Yunnan Province and Burma's Shan states, the American pilots broke up a swarm of Japanese air raiders and blasted 15 out of the sky for certain.

Five other enemy planes probably were destroyed in the combat.

The Japanese were on a special 1,000-mile mission, equipped with extra gas tanks and were out to catch the AVG aground. Twice, however, the heavily gunned Japanese Zero fighters fell into an ambush in the clouds.

THE WAITING YANKS raked them with a savage fire and Japanese planes hurtled from the skies, trailing clouds of white smoke to plunge flaming into paddyfields and verdant jungle growths.

None of the American fliers was lost.

A Texan, who was a Royal Air Force sergeant pilot in Canada after washing-out at the U.S. Air Crops Training School at Love Field, Dallas, Tex., had the closest call.

During the course of the melee he got on the tail of a Zero fighter and, because of the difficulty he'd had confirming five previous combat victims in Burma, he followed his adversary down until he saw him crash in flames.

While the Texan was thus engaged, another Japanese plane got on his tail and sent a burst of machine gun fire through his instrument board. Oil from a broken line spurted over the Texan, blinding him, and he made a crash landing.

As he sat in his wrecked plane, half stunned, another enemy plane swooped low, blazing guns, and narrowly missed finishing him off.

***

WEDNESDAY NOON (April 8) a fast twin-engined Japanese reconnaissance bomber, possibly a Heinkel or JU-88

(German) model scouted the field and eluded two pursuing American fliers flying with throttles wide open. Then, in mid-afternoon, a Japanese fighter formation was reported en route.

Squadron Leader Arvid Olson, of Chicago, and Bob Little, of Seattle, just arrived from Sinogo, went aloft with Ed Overend, of Coronado, Calif., Johnny Donovan, of Montgomery, Ala., R.T. Smith, of Lincoln, Neb., Fritz Wold, of Shawano, Wisc., Cliff Groh, of Chicago, and Fred Hodges, of Memphis, Tenn., at the controls of the older planes.

The Japanese suddenly swooped over the runway, but there were no rows of stationary aircraft. They combed the edges of the field, hunting for concealed prey.

Nearly five miles high in the cloud-patched sky, more of the enemy hovered. Then the Americans counter-attacked!

Brown streaks of lightning dived at the low-flying strafers. Above the scream of motors and cracking gunfire, stricken Japanese planes sounded like exploding bombs when they crashed to the ground.

The Japanese cruising high in the sky stayed there, just dim silver specks to ground observers, while one after another, 10 of their mates died fighting, and the remainder broke and fled in their damaged ships.

Wednesday's score was Olson one and Donovan one, their first victories; Overend, Groh, Hodges, and Little, one apiece, and Smith and Wold, two each.

Hodges' pretty bride of six days, the former Helen Anderson, of Rangoon, saw from a hilltop the lanky Tennessean's triumph of the air.

***

JAPANESE AIR ACTIVITY the following day dropped off to the point where only one reconnaissance wandered into the defensive zone.

Today (Friday, April 10) at dawn, Japanese Navy Zero planes sneaked over the Chinese hills and roared toward the Americans' field in a technique apparently borrowed from the American fliers' devastating attacks on Moulmein and Chiengmai.

Mechanic Dan Keller, of Pittsburgh, and Robert A. Smith, of Oneonta, N.Y.,were warming up Curtis planes and dived for the nearest ditch, bullets nearly dusting their khaki jeans.

Up and down the field, twisting and swerving like playful porpoises, the Japanese emptied their guns. They headed for their base, seemingly reluctant, for they turned and came back for a farewell sweep before vanishing.

But not a single Allied plane on the ground had been burned.

"The worst marksmanship we ever heard of," said Olson, with great relief. "The Japs should take another lesson from Bill Reed and Ken Hernstedt at Moulmein."

THIS AFTERNOON the Japanese returned—in confident buzzing V formations of three planes each—stalking two miles up in puffy thick clouds for the kill. Possibly they expected to find a maimed American Volunteer Group helpless aground.

They tested their guns and made ready to dive.

Then what must be the Japanese pilots' idea of hell broke loose—machine guns firing from above and behind their tails with heavy tracers and armor-piercing bullets slashing at the unarmored navy Zeros.

Bob Keeton, a former blocking halfback in Colorado

collegiate football, Bob Brouk, of Cicero, Ill., and big Bob Smith were drawing first blood.

Smoke geysered from a crashing Japanese plane midway up a mountain, another dug into ploughed land beside a river, another burned out of sight across a ridge.

Bill Reed, Marion, Iowa, ace, was practically smothered with hot oil when his oil cap ripped off his windshield, but hit a navy Zero with a tough angle shot and saw it burst into flames.

Then he slipped into a cloud bank to escape pursuing enemy craft and flew by instruments. "Get ready in case of fire," he radioed Olson, who was calling signals at the communications shack. "I'm coming in to land covered with oil."

Another message came almost immediately from Smith: "Hey, if anybody isn't doing anything, come over here–three Zeros, east of the river."

JAP PIE IN THE SKY

(Chicago Daily 1942 news article)

American airmen who resigned from our Army Air Corps to become honorary Chinamen so that they could pot-shot Jap bombers when we were neutrals, have earned high praise from our Chinese allies. "The most efficient combat group in the world today," is the way they rate with the Chinese leader at Kunming on the Burma Road, where they recently shot down four big Japanese bombers without having their own paint scratched.

These boys are certainly not using the most up-to-date equipment, as their machines were shipped to China months ago. They are meeting and beating Jap fliers in planes built with the help of German technicians on the Messerschmitt 109 and 110 designs.

To them, that stuff is just more pie in the sky.

–The Chicago Daily News 1942

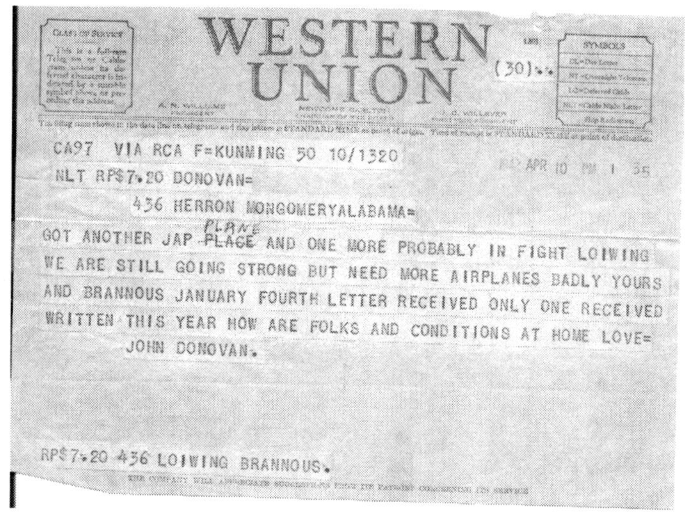

WESTERN UNION (30)

CA97 VIA RCA F=KUNMING 50 10/1320 APR 10 PM 1 35

NLT RP$7.20 DONOVAN=

436 HERRON MONGOMERYALABAMA=

GOT ANOTHER JAP ~~PLACE~~ PLANE AND ONE MORE PROBABLY IN FIGHT LOIWING WE ARE STILL GOING STRONG BUT NEED MORE AIRPLANES BADLY YOURS AND BRANNOUS JANUARY FOURTH LETTER RECEIVED ONLY ONE RECEIVED WRITTEN THIS YEAR HOW ARE FOLKS AND CONDITIONS AT HOME LOVE=

JOHN DONOVAN.

RP$7.20 436 LOIWING BRANNOUS.

John's telegram home, April 10, 1942

Photo courtesy of Brad Smith, son of 3rd Squadron pilot R.T. Smith

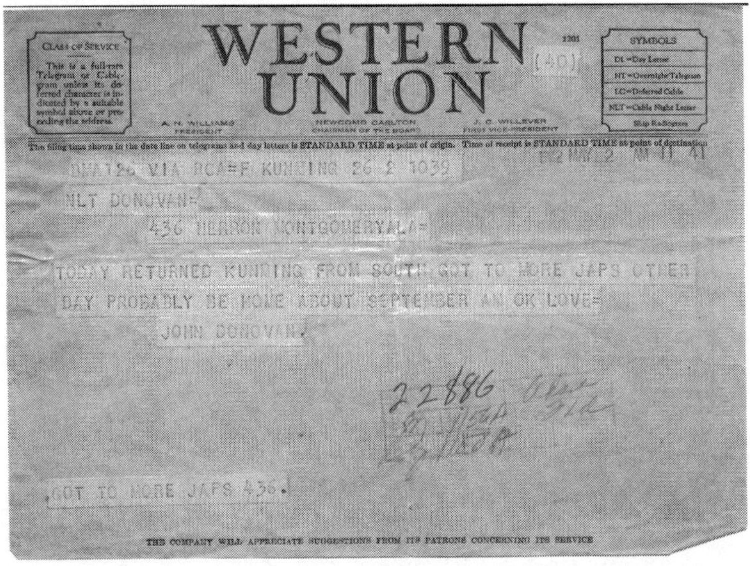

CLASS OF SERVICE

This is a full-rate Telegram or Cablegram unless its deferred character is indicated by a suitable symbol above or preceding the address.

WESTERN UNION

1201

(40)

SYMBOLS

DL = Day Letter

NT = Overnight Telegram

LC = Deferred Cable

NLT = Cable Night Letter

Ship Radiogram

A. N. WILLIAMS, PRESIDENT · NEWCOMB CARLTON, CHAIRMAN OF THE BOARD · J. C. WILLEVER, FIRST VICE-PRESIDENT

The filing time shown in the date line on telegrams and day letters is STANDARD TIME at point of origin. Time of receipt is STANDARD TIME at point of destination

1942 MAY 2 AM 11 41

[illegible]A126 VIA RCA=F KUNMING 26 2 1039

NLT DONOVAN=

436 HERRON MONTGOMERYALA=

TODAY RETURNED KUNMING FROM SOUTH GOT TO MORE JAPS OTHER DAY PROBABLY BE HOME ABOUT SEPTEMBER AM OK LOVE=

JOHN DONOVAN.

GOT TO MORE JAPS 436.

THE COMPANY WILL APPRECIATE SUGGESTIONS FROM ITS PATRONS CONCERNING ITS SERVICE

John's telegram home May 2, 1942 (10 days before death)

TODAY RETURNED KUNMING FROM SOUTH GOT TO MORE JAPS OTHER DAY PROBABLY BE HOME AROUND SEPTEMBER AM OK LOVE

JOHN DONOVAN

This telegram reflects his decision to go home and not stay in the fight in China. Perhaps to rejoin the Navy. We will never know his exact intentions.

23. GERMAN SISTERS

In this letter John writes of a day-long adventure in which he has a great time visiting the "Slave School" run by German sisters. It's not a slave school at all; rather,it's a safe haven for girls who had been slaves and were saved by the sisters. Families too poor to feed their children often sold them for several Chinese dollars, which amounted to only about one American dollar. Their life in slavery usually turned out to be miserable, sometimes brutal, and they almost always became the part-time mistress of the one who bought them. The school was their salvation. There were forty residents who were loved, cared for, and taught to sew and knit by these German sisters.

The Blind School, which John had hoped to visit someday, was established in May 1929 by the "German Sisters of Charity" missionaries. Before moving to Nanning, they had been located close to the American Consulate in the North end of Kunming. Although the children were blind, they were taught how to perform necessary daily tasks and also how to knit and crochet. Approximately seventy-five children lived at The Blind School, with ages ranging from seven to twenty-five. Most were blind from birth, but a few had suffered severe beatings that caused their blindness.

In this lengthy letter, John mentions the old Chinese tradition of binding of little girls' feet—breaking the toes, folding them under the foot, then wrapping the foot in bandages—so that eventually the foot would be shaped into a three-inch lotus. Their belief was the lotus shape was a status symbol and the only way for a woman to marry into money. The practice of binding was banned in 1912. However, many secretly continued to bind their own feet, believing it would provide them with a wealthy husband and a good life. Disfiguring their feet actually destined them to a tragic life, as they were unable to work in the fields picking vegetables and fruit or in the work place.

John tells of parking outside a walled town. The Chinese began to build walls around their villages in the 15th century and were quite successful with towers, moats and gates to block aggressors on the ground. Most were quite elaborate masonry structures built with minimal implements. But the walls were no defense against the Japanese bombers.

This would be John's last travelogue about the people and places he had encountered for the past eight months. When John wasn't fighting the Japanese, his days off were spent traveling the countryside by car, train, or bicycle—he was never at a loss to discover something that would help others see China through the eyes of this tiger.

Kunming, China
May 9, 1942

Dearest Folks,

Yesterday I had a most interesting experience.

There are in this area 10 or 12 German "Sisters." They are part of the Inland Mission organization. Though they are called "Sisters" they are Protestant missionaries.

The organization in which they were originally trained has some German name. But here in China they operate as a part of the China Inland Mission which has missionaries of many different denominations.

You probably have read about their work in Nicol Smith's "Burma Road."

The first time that I encountered them was yesterday. "Red" Petach, wife of one of the pilots and nurse for the AVG, had contacted them some time ago. She had brought some samples to the hostel showing the fine work that was done in linen embroidery by the girls of the "Slave School" which is operated by the German Sisters. Several pilots had placed orders for tablecloths, napkins, etc.

As I will probably be leaving for Chunking shortly, I went down to the French hospital where their office is to see how they were progressing with the work.

Then I began to learn how little I had used my native curiosity here in Kunming. Usually, if there is anything of interest around a place I am prone to investigate.

There were two Sisters at the hospital. One is an expert dentist. She had one patient in the chair and several waiting. The other, Sister Caroline, is the secretary, banker, "head" of their own organization. Both were extremely nice and very friendly.

It turned out that both the "Blind School" and "Slave School" had some time ago been moved out of Kunming because of the dangers from bombing. Also, many air raid alarms had resulted in the girls spending most of many days in ditches, thereby not getting any work done.

I was off for the day because of being on night "alert." I suggested that I would be glad to drive out into the country and see the school and how the work was done. Sister Caroline then informed me that the "Slave School" was composed of girls who were formerly sold into slavery by their parents, and had been so mistreated by their owners that the attention of the Sisters had been called to the matter and the Sisters had taken all they could and put them into this school—which they call the "Girl's Industrial School," was now located at Oshan, some 150 Kilometers from Kunming.

In order to get to this school one could drive as far as Ushee and then walk for five hours. I had neither the time nor the inclination for the walk. Several of the Sisters had walked this distance to and from Kunming.

We discussed several possibilities of getting to Oshan to get the table covers, etc. She felt that much of the work was ready. Of course, there was no telephone either to Oshan or Ushee. Then she suggested that she send Ammah (Chinese maid) by train to a town that is about a third of the distance and that the Ammah could walk the rest of the way. At Oshan the goods could be brought by mule pack or coolies.

Sister Caroline felt sure that the Sisters at Oshan had already sent some of the orders to the Sisters at Ushee, which is about 110 kilometers from Kunming.

I offered to drive to Ushee as that seemed an excellent way to spend the day. Immediately she wanted to know if she might go along. I was most agreeable to this as Sister Caroline was a most enjoyable person and the day was a most enjoyable day.

Sister Athelia, the dentist, would like to have gone but felt that she should stay and take care of her patients.

It was about 10 in the morning and one of those mornings that is refreshing, cool, everything is bright and all the trees and fields are very green.

When I offered her some chewing gum and she had to be told what it was, since she had never tasted any, I knew right away that I had with me a girl unlike most.

She was as happy about getting a chance to go and see the other Sisters at Ushee and driving through the country, instead of having to ride a smelly Chinese bus which are old and overcrowded, that she seemed more like an excited 10 year old. She was really a gay person to be with. When we stopped at the covered bridge that spanned a particularly beautiful creek, she felt that I was being too kind when I took her picture. She had learned to drive while in China but did not know how to operate the steering wheel gear shift on the station wagon that we were in.

Apparently the Sisters are having a difficult time since their money from Germany has been cut off for a couple of years. Also, funds from the United States have been held up. Consequently the Sisters themselves have had to live frugally, eating only one full meal a day and that mostly rice. She was most appreciative for our placing orders for some of the hand made work from the school.

Being Germans, the Sisters have had to be very careful lest they arouse suspicion, though they have been in China eight or ten years or more. Though they have been bombed out of different places and have worked with the Chinese, doctoring and nursing them, and doing charity and religious work, they have to live a more or less confined life, instead of being able to enjoy some of the honor and respect which is their due.

Sister Caroline related how she happened to become a “Deaconess” or Sister, saying that she was still glad she had done so. She has three sisters, four brothers, and four brothers-in-law still in Germany, as well as her mother. Yet she has had no word from any of them in over two years.

The road to Ushee was a good road, as Chinese roads go. I doubt if I would have been able to find the way alone. During the first part of the trip the road skirted the lake and then climbed into the mountains. We passed many old walled towns. A “Jing Baws” was on shortly after we left Kunming as anyone could see because the population of the towns and villages were scattering to the hills. I felt certain that there would be no harm for us, for if the Japs did get to Kunming they would be more interested in the aerodrome and factories than towns and villages–though I have known this not to be true. Anyway, "Jing Baws" are only recurring incidents which anyone in this part of the world gets accustomed to, so we forgot about Japanese airplanes and thoroughly enjoyed the trip, which was as much fun for me as it was for Sister Caroline.

She explained points of interest along the road. When I inquired about a fairly large temple located outside one of the walled towns, she explained that for several generations some of the richest parents in the town had regularly sacrificed their babies at this temple in order to satisfy the evil spirits. Doing this they consider an honor. Now, however, they slaughter hogs, cattle, and chickens.

During the latter part of the trip we got more into "the country." Whenever people or horses on the road heard our car coming they would run wildly out into the fields. Here, all the women's feet were bound. In Kunming only half the women's feet are bound. If we stop the car in a village, we were immediately the center of attention for the entire population. They would inspect the car and stand gaping at us. Sister Caroline always took pride in telling that I was a Manquorun who came to China to "da erbon faygie" (fight Japanese warplanes). She speaks Chinese as her second tongue, as well as perfect English and French.

After about two and a half hours we reached Ushee. Since the streets are not wide enough for automobiles, we had to leave the station wagon outside the walls. It was market-day and the town and narrow streets were filled with people.

Unless you have been to "the country" to visit relatives who are particularly fond of you, you cannot imagine how tickled the four Sisters at Ushee were when they saw us walk in. Like people in another generation in the South were always glad to see strangers because of their "news value," the Sisters were thirsting for news, and were happy to see another white person. More than that, a visit from an AVG member carried a deeper meaning. Written on all our cars in Chinese is the fact that we are the AVG. By paying a friendly visit to them they gained "face" in the eyes of the Chinese population of the town, some of whom have booed or laughed at them when they have walked on the streets.

As we were hungry, it was not long before there was ample good Chinese chow spread before us. All the Sisters were rather young and seemed in good spirits. One of the Sisters, Elsie, had an excellent sense of humor. She brought out some kind of wine she had made, and it was very good. I suppose it was more fruit punch than wine.

There was a few doors away a Mr. and Mrs. Wolf, missionaries, and their daughter, Elizabeth, age four. These were the only other white people for miles around. Elizabeth was a very pretty child, and I enjoyed playing with her. One of the Sisters had gone to fetch them as they felt that the Wolfs (NOT Wolves) would feel bad if visitors had come and they had not met them.

All of us sat around and discussed their work, the war, etc. Sister Lena was the "doctor." She said that an average of forty patients per day came into the clinic. The word clinic should have had quotation marks, too, for it was nothing more than a bare room with a few benches and limited equipment and supplies.

I had observed several people wearing colored pieces of paper pasted on each side of their forehead. Sister Lena explained that this was to cure them of trachoma or headache, so the Chinese thought. I mean by this that this was a Chinese remedy—not Sister Lena's.

There was a blind girl there. She did excellent knitting.

Samples of her work were for sale. There were sweaters, children's dresses, etc.

One of the Sisters had been at Ushee for five years and had only been as far as Kunming three times during that period.

I learned much about the Sister's work; the many ways in which they try to help the Chinese; their own homesickness for their native Germany.

I say that one has to see and be around the Chinese to learn that any ordinary person from the U.S., England, Germany, or any modern industrialized country, can teach them many things. Many Chinese are completely lacking in the most rudimentary things that any child at home would know. The Chinese (in most cases) are so completely lacking in assuming responsibility; have a very poor knack at understanding anything mechanical; will wait three hours for a coolie to get a basket of vegetables into the house, whereas they could have moved the basket inside in three minutes. What I have said probably applies to 80% of the Chinese in its entirety and only partly applies to the rest.

If you have "stuck" with me this far, your patience is greater than your criticism.

Their house was very well constructed and, of course, spotlessly clean. There was no electricity in the town. They used oil lamps at night. Water has to be carried some distance, and all of it has to be boiled before drinking.

We had planned upon departing early in order to be back so that the night crew could have the car. When we decided to leave all the Sisters and the Wolfs accompanied us back to the town gate and the car. I carried Elizabeth on my shoulders, thereby creating quite a scene on the streets.

You should see the little stores and shops and the frugal wares that they offer for sale. There is no such thing as ice and meat is hung out in front of the shop for flies and filth to accumulate upon it.

Reaching the car, we discovered that one of the tires was flat. There was no spare. The only car owned in Ushee was in Kunming. Let me say it was seven hours later before the tire was fixed, and Sister Caroline and I were on our way to Kunming; and it was well past midnight before we reached there.

However, it was not as bad as it sounds. The extra time spent there was enjoyable. When it became dark the Sisters brought down food and hot coffee and some of the best cakes that I have ever eaten. They stayed around watching the matter of a tube being patched with absorbing interest—so did the 200 Chinese, until the matter became so bad that we had to run as many as we could away.

In the U.S. you have seen a painter or telephone man at work on a main street and observed pedestrians stopping to watch. Well, here in China if someone gets in trouble, has an accident, or is working on a store front, automobile, or sump'n, within a few minutes a crowd of kibitzers, advisors, sympathizers gather. They get in your way, smell bad, and will steal anything left lying around.

Finding a truck which fortunately had patching equipment, I employed the driver to fix the puncture. He fixed it and in putting the tire back on the rim made another puncture. This happened five times. The sixth time I fixed the puncture and in putting the tire on I cut a hole in the tube by pinching it against the rim. Way after dark when the seventh hole was patched the tire was put on successfully and we were ready to go.

Before leaving, we all loaded into the car and took a short ride which was enjoyed by all. Returning to the town, the town gate was locked and the guard had to be awakened to let them in.

I would like to make the trip to Oshan if I can get a couple days off. Also to Nanning where the Blind Girl's School is located.

All of the above happened yesterday.

Did not get much sleep last night and have been on "alert" since 5 this morning. At seven-thirty this morning twelve of us flew down about 100 miles over the lines and bombed and strafed enemy trucks and a few armored cars. Right in the middle of one of our former aerodromes was an enemy two-engine observation plane. All of us swooped down and shot it to bits. There has been no other activity today except three fellows that went on a mission a couple of hours ago that I hope they get back from. It was a pretty dangerous mission.

They got back with good results. I have been talking with them and Colonel Chennault a couple hours tonight during and after dinner. It's getting late–past bed time and I expect to see plenty of activity tomorrow–so, since I have to be up at 4:15–Good nite.

P.S. We've got the Japs on the run the past couple of days if we can just keep 'em running.

Love, John Jr.

over the lines and bombed and strafed enemy trucks and a few armored cars. Right in the middle of one of our former aerdromes was an enemy two-engine observation plane. All of us swooped down and shot it to bits. There has been no other activity to-day except three fellows that went on a mission a couple hours ago that I hope they get back from. It is a pretty dangerous mission. They got back OK with good results. I have been talking with them and the Colonel Chennault a couple hours to-nite during and after dinner. It's getting late - past bed time and I expect to see plenty activity to-morrow - so, since I have to be up at 4:15 - Good nite.

P.S. We've got the Japs on the run the past couple days if we can just

Love, John, Jr.

Final addition to John's letter is hand written.

24. YOU MUST NOT FEEL BADLY ABOUT MY DEATH

In this letter, John dictated his message to Chaplain Paul Frillman—just in case—prior to launching a dangerous mission over Japanese-held French Indo-China. It turned out to be his last mission. The sentences are fragmented, certainly not like John wrote his letters. It's almost as if he was rushed to get to his aircraft. It was later transcribed into a telegram and then sent home to his family after Chennault's missing-in-action notification. In John's previous letter only three days before, he mentions the mission flown that day was a dangerous one. It was possible all pilots wrote letters like this, but most did not have to be used.

Mrs. Mary Stella Donovan
436 Herron St. Montgomery, Ala.

Dear Folks, You must not feel badly about my death. The small part that I have played in the war though it has cost me my life, I am glad to give. That life has meant much to me but not so much that I am too distressed at leaving and neither must you be. I had only a few things planned for the future. One of the most important was a nice home. Mamma will please me much if she will live in a more comfortable home with many flowers and trees. I am happy and so must she be.

Love to all,
John Junior

BMA 153 VIA RCA = 7 Kunming 129/119 1/0
27 1025-

N.L.T.
Mrs Mary Stella Donovan
436 Herron St. Montgomery. Ala.

Dear Folks, you must not feel badly about my Death the small part that I have played in the War though it has cost me my life. I am glad to give. that Life has meant much to me but not, so much that I am too distressed at leaving and neither must you be I had only a few things planned for the future one of the most important was a nice home. Mamma will please me much if she will live in a more comfortable home with many flowers and trees. I am happy and so must she be

Love to all

John Junior

The hand-written note John dictated to Paul Frillman prior to John's last mission over Hanoi.

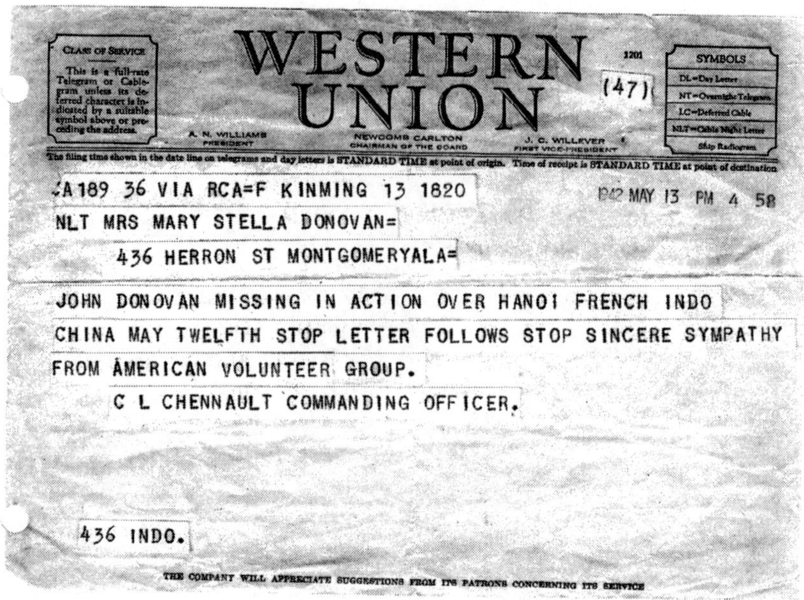

WESTERN UNION

CLASS OF SERVICE
This is a full-rate Telegram or Cablegram unless its deferred character is indicated by a suitable symbol above or preceding the address.

A. N. WILLIAMS PRESIDENT — NEWCOMB CARLTON CHAIRMAN OF THE BOARD — J. C. WILLEVER FIRST VICE-PRESIDENT

SYMBOLS
DL=Day Letter
NT=Overnight Telegram
LC=Deferred Cable
NLT=Cable Night Letter
Ship Radiogram

1201

(47)

The filing time shown in the date line on telegrams and day letters is STANDARD TIME at point of origin. Time of receipt is STANDARD TIME at point of destination

A189 36 VIA RCA=F KINMING 13 1820 — 1942 MAY 13 PM 4 58

NLT MRS MARY STELLA DONOVAN=
436 HERRON ST MONTGOMERYALA=

JOHN DONOVAN MISSING IN ACTION OVER HANOI FRENCH INDO CHINA MAY TWELFTH STOP LETTER FOLLOWS STOP SINCERE SYMPATHY FROM AMERICAN VOLUNTEER GROUP.
C L CHENNAULT COMMANDING OFFICER.

436 INDO.

THE COMPANY WILL APPRECIATE SUGGESTIONS FROM ITS PATRONS CONCERNING ITS SERVICE

Missing in Action telegram from Chennault, May 13, 1942

John's strafing run over the Hanoi airport was chronicled in the newspaper but lacked the report of the death of an American pilot—John Donovan.

> CHUNKING—May 13—(AP) "Flying Tigers" of the American Volunteer Group bombed the Japanese airdrome at Hanoi, Indo-China, yesterday and destroyed 15 grounded planes, AVG headquarters announced today. At least 25 more Japanese planes were damaged and direct hits were scored on administration buildings, a communique said.

Headquarters American Volunteer Group
Office Of The Commanding Officer
Kunming, Yunnan, China
May 18th, 1942

Mrs. Mary Stella Donovan
436 Herron Street
Montgomery, Alabama

Dear Mrs. Donovan,
The following radio message was sent you on May 13th:

"JOHN DONOVAN MISSING IN ACTION OVER HANOI FRENCH INDO-CHINA MAY 12TH STOP LETTER FOLLOWS STOP SINCERE SYMPATHY FROM AMERICAN VOLUNTEER GROUP

(SIGNED) C.L. CHENNAULT
COMMANDING OFFICER

On May 12th, John Donovan went on a volunteer mission down into Hanoi with five other A.V.G. pilots. The enemy strength at Hanoi has always been very great, and it was the object of this mission to reduce that strength before the greater part of it could be moved up to advanced bases and used against us. The mission was entirely successful, but, unfortunately, Donovan was asked to pay the price of another glorious victory for the American Volunteer Group. Fragments from anti-aircraft fire evidently struck his ship, and he was last seen trying to land his ship in enemy territory.

The next day an official recognition from Generalissimo Chiang Kai-Shek reached our office here, and John T. Donovan has been given honorary appointment to a Captaincy in the Chinese Air Force. A personal recognition for bravery and courage from the leader of people, who have been fighting for almost five years for a cause in which they believe, is an honor bestowed only rarely. Our greatest regret is he was not here to receive our congratulations and well wishes.

Donovan left several confidential requests in case of any accident, one of which expressed the desire that his personal effects be sold. We are now making inventories and all monies realized from the sale thereof. As soon as possible, we shall send you a small bag containing his letters, papers and other articles, which he asked me to send to you.

While this information does not absolutely preclude the possibility of your son's safety, it is going to demand a great sacrifice on your part. Until we have more definite information, we can only believe that he did land his plane safely and is not being held in custody by the enemy in Hanoi, French Indo-China. Our intelligence service has orders to search out definite information on his condition and whereabouts, and I assure you that this information, when established, shall be sent on to you immediately.

Our sympathies go out to you at this time. Though we were privileged to know him all too briefly, we shall always remember him with fond respect. His record is one to be proud of, and for us it shall always bear testimony to his bravery and courage.

With sincere sympathy,

C. L. Chennault

C.L. Chennault
Brig. General, U.S.A.

Commanding A.V.G.

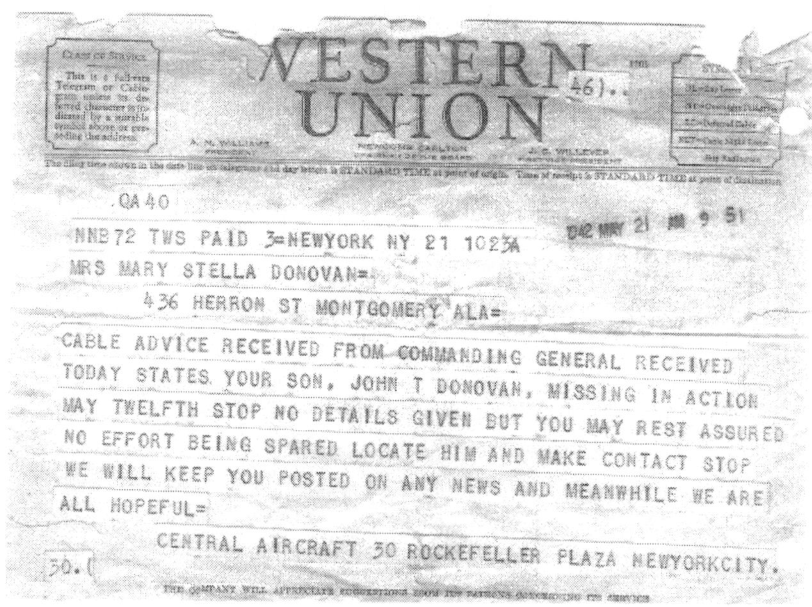

WESTERN UNION

QA 40

NNB72 TWS PAID 3=NEWYORK NY 21 1023A

1942 MAY 21 AM 9 51

MRS MARY STELLA DONOVAN=

436 HERRON ST MONTGOMERY ALA=

CABLE ADVICE RECEIVED FROM COMMANDING GENERAL RECEIVED TODAY STATES YOUR SON, JOHN T DONOVAN, MISSING IN ACTION MAY TWELFTH STOP NO DETAILS GIVEN BUT YOU MAY REST ASSURED NO EFFORT BEING SPARED LOCATE HIM AND MAKE CONTACT STOP WE WILL KEEP YOU POSTED ON ANY NEWS AND MEANWHILE WE ARE ALL HOPEFUL=

CENTRAL AIRCRAFT 30 ROCKEFELLER PLAZA NEWYORKCITY.

30.

Central Aircraft Manufacturing Company telegram, May 21, 1942

Central Aircraft Manufacturing Company
Federal Inc., U.S.A.
Lowing, Yunnan, China

New York Office
30 Rockefeller Plaza

May 21, 1942

Mrs. Mary S. Donovan
436 Herron Street
Montgomery, Alabama

Dear Mrs. Donovan:

We regret exceedingly that we have no definite word to add to the cable about John. However, we are hopeful that he will come through all right. You may be sure that his comrades will not give up on searching for him, and we will make every effort to see if the International Red Cross can establish some sort of contact. They are endeavoring to do this in a few other cases, and while the procedure is necessarily slow, due to the distances involved, and the hazards of communication, we nevertheless know that they exert every effort to locate anyone missing. Therefore, may we ask you to be of good cheer, and we will communicate with you immediately if we have anything to report.

Faithfully yours,
Alice H. Leonard
AHL/mm(Mrs.) Alice H. Leonard

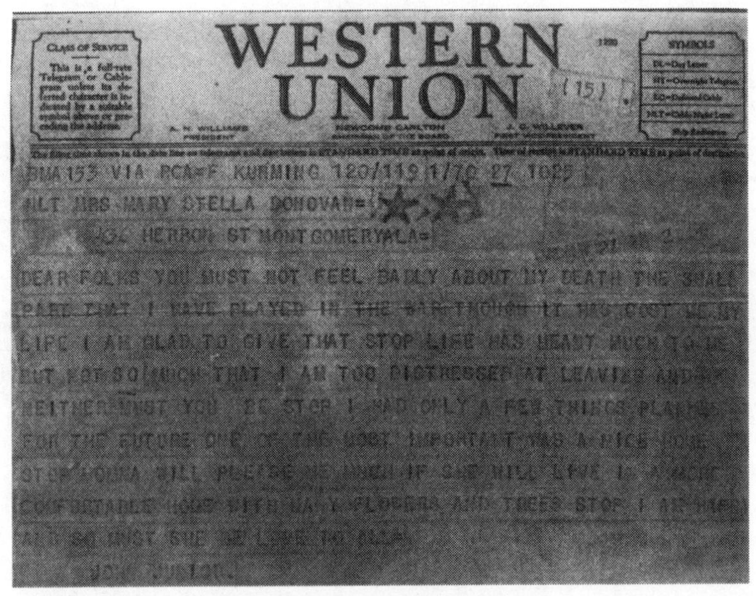

WESTERN UNION

(15)

[illegible] VIA RCA=F KUNMING 120/119 1/70 27 [illegible]

NLT MRS MARY STELLA DONOVAN=

[illegible] HERRON ST MONTGOMERYALA=

DEAR FOLKS YOU MUST NOT FEEL BADLY ABOUT MY DEATH THE SMALL PART THAT I HAVE PLAYED IN THE WAR THOUGH IT HAS COST ME MY LIFE I AM GLAD TO GIVE THAT STOP LIFE HAS MEANT MUCH TO ME BUT NOT SO MUCH THAT I AM TOO DISTRESSED AT LEAVING AND NEITHER MUST YOU BE STOP I HAD ONLY A FEW THINGS PLANNED FOR THE FUTURE ONE OF THE MOST IMPORTANT WAS A NICE HOME STOP MOMMA WILL PLEASE ME MUCH IF SHE WILL LIVE IN A MORE COMFORTABLE HOME WITH MANY FLOWERS AND TREES STOP I AM HAPPY AND SO MUST SHE BE LOVE TO ALL

JOHN DONOVAN.

The letter John dictated to Chaplain Frillman arrives via telegram in Montgomery May 27, 1942

WESTERN UNION

CA67 VIA RCA=F KUNMING 27 MAY 26 0150=

LC MRS MARY STELLA DONOVAN=

436 HERRON ST MONTGOMERYALA=

942 MAY 27 PM 12 25

DEFINITELY CONFIRMED JOHN TYLER DONOVAN KILLED IN ACTION AT HANOI FRENCH INDOCHINA MAY TWELFTH STOP LETTER FOLLOWS STOP SINCERE SYMPATH FROM AMERICAN VOLUNTEER GROUP=

CL CHENNAULT COMMANDING OFFICER.

436 HANOI CL KUNMING

May 27, 1942, KIA confirmation telegram arrives in Alabama.

Headquarters American Volunteer Group
Office Of The Commanding Officer
Kunming, Yunnan, China
May 30th, 1942

Mrs. Mary Stella Donovan
436 Herron Street
Montgomery, Alabama

Dear Mrs. Donovan,

On May 27th, we sent you the following radio message:

"DEFINITELY CONFIRMED JOHN TYLER DONOVAN KILLED IN ACTION AT HANOI FRENCH INDO-CHINA, MAY 12TH STOP LETTER FOLLOWS STOP SINCERE SYMPATHY FROM AMERICAN VOLUNTEER GROUP.

(SIGNED) C.L. CHENNAULT
COMMANDING OFFICER

Our radio message of May 12th gave you the information that John Donovan was missing after a mission over Hanoi. Since that time we have had a confirmed report that he was killed on that date over enemy territory. Fragments from ground fire struck his ship, forcing him to try to land his disabled ship. He crashed with his ship and died in his plane.

In accordance with his wishes, all his personal effects, with the exception of some gifts which he wanted sent home to you, have been sold at auction sale, and all monies realized from there have already been deposited with our Finance Office to be credited to his estate through our New York Office. You may look for a substantial deposit from them in the near future. Just as soon as our part of his estate has been completely settled here, we shall send you all the information regarding inventories, sales, and deposits made toward his estate.

The American Volunteer Group regrets very deeply the loss of John Donovan and asks to be included always in the memories of the son you gave for a cause in which we still believe and for which we are fighting even now.

With sincere sympathy,

C. L. Chennault
C.L. Chennault
Brig. General, U.S.A.
Commanding A.V.G.

INVENTORY------PERSONAL EFFECTS OF JOHN TYLER DONOVAN

ALL SOLD OUTRIGHT OR AT AUCTION

OUTRIGHT

1 Pr. Blue Striped Trousers
1 Blue Sport Coat
1 Pin-Striped Suit (3 Piece)m
2 Wool Service Trousers
1 Khaki Service Trousers
1 Grey Suit (2 Piece)
1 Phillips Radio (Small Table Model)
1 Large Radio (Table Model)
1 Dressing Gown
1 Black Val-Pak
1 Pr. Tennis Shoes
1 Pr. White Shoes
2 Prs. Toungoo Boots
1 Pr. Brown Shoes
2 --15 yd. Belts Cretonne Cloth
3½ yds. Gabardine Uniform Material
1 Toilet Kit
1 Portable Remington Typewrite r
1 Small Week-end Bag
1 Military Cap
1 Wardrobe Trunk
2 Silver Loving Cups
1 Scarf
4 Pillows
1 Bathmat
2 Gold-embroideree Bedspreads
3 Embroidered Tapestries
3 Sheets
1 .22 Calibre Rifle with 200 Rds. Ammunition
1 Kodak--116 Vigilant
1 Still Camera---127 Acro
1 Funk and Wagnalls College Dictionary
1 Photographic Album
1 Desert Hat
7 Tea Sets--Service for Six
3 Neckties
2 Khaki Shirts
2 Dress Shirts
5 Sport Shirts
2 Prs. Pajamas
5 Prs. Sox
8 Undershirts
1 Sweatshirt
6 Handkerchiefs
1 Web Belt
3 Bath Towels

OTHER ASSETS

Received from J.E? Petach--------C.N.$300.00
Bank Drafts
Two C.N.$1000 Bonds
Bank Deposits

SOLD AT AUCTION

1 Gent's Utility Case
1 Mirror
1 Shoe-shining Kit
1 Pr. Goggles and Case
3 Bottles South African Brandy
1 Tin Mechanic'sxSoap
4 --1 lb. Tins Prince Albert Tobacco
3 Small Tins English Smoking Mixture
1 Carton Players Cigarettes
1 Roll Super XX Film
2 Small Carved Elephants
1 Small Zipper Bag
3 Small Tins Edgeworth Tobacco
1 Javanese Wood-carved Head
1 Garrison Cap
1 Rubber Blanket
1 Val-Pak
19 Bottles Stout
1 Small Bottle Angostura Bitters

(NOTE! THE SALE OF THESE EFFECTS REALIZED RUPEES 1207/-/-)

As per John's request, most items were sold at auction—even his typewriter. The money raised from the auction was sent home to his mother.

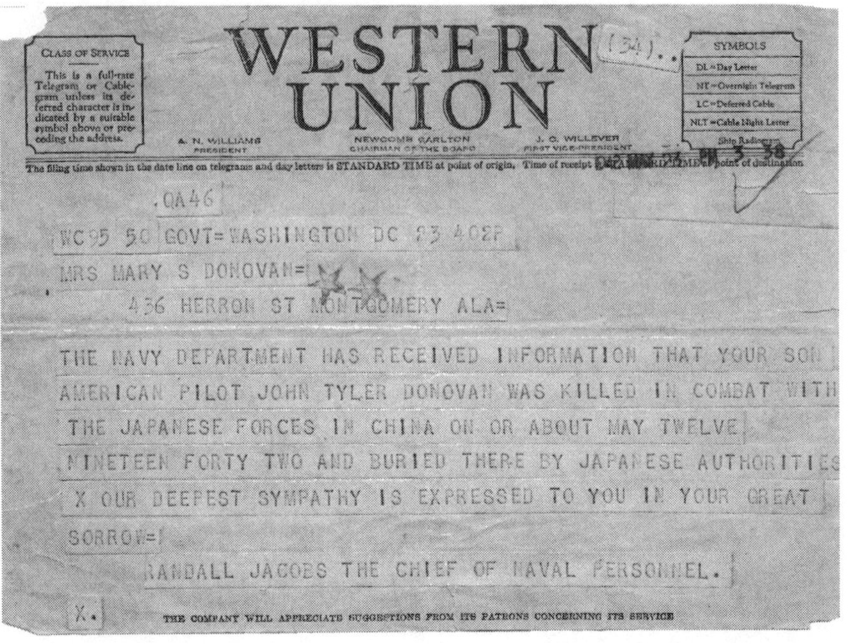

WESTERN UNION

.QA46

WC95 50 GOVT=WASHINGTON DC 23 402P

MRS MARY S DONOVAN=

436 HERRON ST MONTGOMERY ALA=

THE NAVY DEPARTMENT HAS RECEIVED INFORMATION THAT YOUR SON AMERICAN PILOT JOHN TYLER DONOVAN WAS KILLED IN COMBAT WITH THE JAPANESE FORCES IN CHINA ON OR ABOUT MAY TWELVE NINETEEN FORTY TWO AND BURIED THERE BY JAPANESE AUTHORITIES X OUR DEEPEST SYMPATHY IS EXPRESSED TO YOU IN YOUR GREAT SORROW=

RANDALL JACOBS THE CHIEF OF NAVAL PERSONNEL.

THE COMPANY WILL APPRECIATE SUGGESTIONS FROM ITS PATRONS CONCERNING ITS SERVICE

Telegram from Chief of Naval Personnel May 23, 1942

Form No. 192
FOREIGN SERVICE
(Corrected August 1938)

AMERICAN FOREIGN SERVICE

REPORT OF THE DEATH OF AN AMERICAN CITIZEN

Consult Sections XIII-7 and XIII-8 and Notes of the Foreign Service Regulations

Kunming(Yunnanfu), China, May 27, 1942.
(Place and date)

Name in full: John Tyler Donovan Age: 27;Born Apr.30,1915 (As nearly as can be ascertained)

Native or naturalized: Native Occupation: Airplane pilot

Date of death: May (Month) 12 (Day) late afternoon (Hour) (Minute) 1942 (Year)

Place of death: Hanoi Aerodrome, (Number and street) or (Hospital or hotel) Hanoi, (City) French Indochina (Country)

Cause of death: Shot down while making air raid on Hanoi Aerodrome, according to statement of Paul W. Frillmann, Chaplain, First American Volunteer Group. (Include authority for statement)

Disposition of the remains: Not known

Local law as to disinterring remains: Not known

Disposition of the effects: Inventoried by Robert Prescott, AVG. Small personal effects to be sent to next of kin. Other effects auctioned and money realized to be credited to deceased's estate.

Person or official responsible for custody of effects and accounting therefor: Supply Officer, First American Volunteer Group.

Accompanied by relatives or friends as follows:

NAME	ADDRESS	RELATIONSHIP

Address of relatives (so far as known):

	NAME	ADDRESS	RELATIONSHIP
1.	Mrs. Mary Stella Donovan,	436 Herron St., Montgomery, Ala.,	Mother
2.			

Notification sent to:

Mrs. Mary Stella Donovan (Name) by telegraph (Mail or telegraph) on May 26, 1942 (Date)

Mrs. Mary Stella Donovan (Name) by mail (Mail or telegraph) on May 27, 1942 (Date)

This information and data concerning an inventory of the effects, accounts, etc., have been placed under File 330 in the correspondence of this office.

Remarks: Deceased's passport No. 702240(U7966) issued by the Department of State at Washington on August 13, 1941 cancelled and placed in this Consulate's files.

Troy L. Perkins,
Consul of the United States of America.

[SEAL]

No fee prescribed.

(To be sent *in duplicate* to the Department of State. To be forwarded *in triplicate* when decedent is an American-citizen seaman, a pensioner, or a Veterans Administration or Social Security beneficiary.

Document courtesy of Kelleen Donovan Thornock

25. HANOI, FRENCH INDO-CHINA

The Chinese Minister of Foreign Affairs, (Tse-Ven) Soong, wrote the condolence letter below to John's mother. T.V. is considered one of the initiators of the American Volunteer Group and worked tirelessly in Washington, D.C., on behalf of Generalissimo Chiang Kai-shek.

In addition, T.V. was instrumental in developing the concept for the AVG's logo of the tiger with wings. In Hollywood, California, Walt Disney Studios created the logo and sent almost one hundred vinyl decals to apply to all the aircraft. The shark's mouth on the nose of the P-40 had nothing to do with the "Flying Tiger." It just made the planes appear ferocious—like a shark. A shark's mouth on an airplane was seen by one of the pilots in "India Illustrated Weekly" magazine and was originally planned for just his squadron. Chennault only gave the go-ahead if all the squadrons were painted alike.

T.V.'s concept is mentioned in author Martha Byrd's book, "Chennault: Giving Wings to the Tiger." Byrd wrote, "Soong then invoked the Chinese saying, 'Giving wings to the tiger.' He reminded them that the tiger was the most formidable animal alive, but when endowed with wings its prowess was super-colossal."

Interestingly, T.V. was Madame Chiang Kai-shek's brother, and he too was educated in the United States. After the war, he became an extremely wealthy businessman, served as a politician, and later left China. He settled in San Francisco where he lived quietly until his death in 1971.

Following the heartfelt letter from T.V. Soong, is a letter from Chennault. He sends his deepest sympathy but also tells Stella that John's loss "was as much a blow to me as if I had lost one of my own sons."

The final letter is from Stella to the French Ambassador with a plea for his assistance to help locate John's grave following the end of the war.

May 30, 1942

Mrs. Mary Stella Donovan
436 Herron Street
Montgomery, Alabama

Dear Mrs. Donovan,

It is with deep regret that I have learned of the death of your son, John Tyler Donovan, who died in combat against the Japanese over Hanoi, Indo-China, on May 12, 1942.

Your son was one of a group of brave and farsighted young men who sensed the danger, not only to China but to America and to freedom throughout the world, in the ruthless and predatory course of Japanese militarism. Not waiting to be called, this group went forward to meet the enemy, prepared to sacrifice themselves, if need be, in order that the democracies might gain precious time, that freedom might live, that countless other lives might be saved.

The record already made by the American Volunteer Group in aerial combat against the Japanese is one of which every American may be proud. Although this may be of small comfort to you, in view of your son's sacrifice, perhaps it will help you to feel that he met death as I am sure he would have wanted to meet it—in quick and valiant action against an enemy not only of China, but also of his own country.

You may have heard that the American Volunteer Group has adopted as its emblem, a "Flying Tiger." The figure chosen was designed by The Walt Disney Studios and shows a winged tiger leaping out of a victory "V." It will be worn as a lapel insignia by your son's comrades and will also appear in color on the fuselage of each plane. As a tribute to your son's memory, I have the honor to send you, under separate cover, a gold replica of the insignia, which he so richly deserved.

As Foreign Minister of the Republic of China, I want to express to you, on behalf of my countrymen and of Generalissimo Chiang Kai-shek personally, the sense of honor which is ours that your son saw fit to give his life in China for the cause of freedom. Like Lafayette in America, these gallant young men will forever be gratefully enshrined in the memory of the Chinese people.

Very truly yours,

T. V. Soong
Minister for Foreign Affairs
Of the Republic of China

Headquarters American Volunteer Group
Office Of The Commanding Officer

July 22, 1942

Mary Stella Donovan
Montgomery, Alabama

Dear Mrs. Donovan:

Replying to your letter of June 4, I am very sorry that my letter promised by radio has not reached you. I am sure that you have received it by now and that its long delay was due to war conditions.

In answer to your questions, I regret to inform you that there can no longer be any doubt about John being killed at Hanoi, Indo-China. The reason that I informed you that he was missing was in order to investigate the possibility that he might have survived the crash of his airplane. I am not permitted to tell you how I received positive information that he had been buried in a cemetery at Hanoi, but I assure you that my information is reliable and must be accepted at this time.

I believe that there is an excellent chance of locating his grave after the war, and if desired, returning his body to the States. I do not believe that very much could be done now due to the fact that Hanoi is controlled by the Japanese though still officially French territory. It is barely possible, however, that an appeal to the French Ambassador at Washington might result in an effort to mark the grave permanently if nothing more. John was a particular favorite of mine, and his loss was as much a blow to me as if I had lost one of my own sons. I would not have permitted him to go on the mission if I had not believed that it was relatively safe for all the pilots, and I have never been able to understand how his plane was hit while none of the others received a single bullet hole. It must have been due to his excessive zeal, which caused him to fly too low and so run into a burst of enemy fire. I can assure you that he died with his face to the enemy and with his machine guns flaming a challenge to the enemies of our country.

If there is anything else that I can do for you, please do not hesitate to call upon me. With my deepest sympathy, I am,

Most sincerely,
C.L. Chennault
C.L.CHENNAULT
Brigadier General. A.U.S.,
Commanding
CLC/tgt

Honorable Gaston Henri-Haye
French Embassy
Washington, D.C.

Sir:

I am addressing you about a subject which has no relationship to the changing wind of international relations, but which is universal through all times and all peoples: the concern of a mother over a son who was killed in action and who lies, so far as she knows, in an unmarked grave.

On May 12, 1942, my son, John Donovan, Jr., a former Ensign in the United States Navy, was killed in action while flying with the American Volunteer Group. I am informed by Brigadier General C.L. Chennault, who was in command of the AVG, that John's death occurred while he was on a mission against the Japanese concentration at Hanoi, French Indo-China. Through sources known only to him, General Chennault has informed me that it has been definitely established that John was buried in a cemetery in that city.

This is all I know.

Is it possible that through your good offices, members of the French Diplomatic Service at Hanoi might arrange to permanently mark this grave? A marker which would last at least for the duration of the war would give me a great deal of comfort and make it possible for me to make some appropriate arrangements after the war is over.

I am not familiar with all of the ramifications of diplomatic relations today, but I can assure you that I will be eternally indebted to France should it be possible for you to perform this simple service.

Respectfully,

(Mrs.) Mary Stella Donovan
436 Herron Street
Montgomery, Alabama

26. BURIED AT THE EDGE OF THE FIELD

Two people who knew John well in China, Chaplin Frillman, who John dictated his final request to, and fellow AVG pilot Bob Prescott, returned to the States in August. The Chaplin responds to two letters from Stella and embellishes John's burial to comfort her. Together, Frillman and Prescott had fulfilled John's request of selling most of his personal items and to bring what John specified to his mother.

Bob was more than just a fellow pilot to John, they had followed a similar path in life. They enlisted together in California, flew together in Pensacola, and resigned together to join the American Volunteer Group. They spent 48 days on the Boschfontein together. They fought the Japanese in the best of times and the worst of times. Now, in a final gesture of respect to his friend and fallen comrade, Prescott traveled to Alabama to bring the gifts John had purchased for his family.

August 15, 1942
Maywood, Illinois

Mrs. M.S. Donovan
436 Herron Street

Montgomery, Alabama

Dear Mrs. Donovan;

Your letters of July 28 and Aug.11 have reached me here in Maywood, Ill. I want to tell you how sorry I am not to have answered sooner. I have been in Washington for some time, and have also spent some days in West Virginia, but I do now have time to write and tell you all I know.

You ask about John's burial and the burial place. We are led to believe that John was buried right at the airfield at Hanoi. This information reached us over Japanese radio, telling us that they buried the A.V.G. pilot who crashed over the airfield with all military honors. Now this could only have been John. I, personally, cannot give you any more information regarding the actual location of the grave, but we believe he was buried right on the edge of the Japanese field located at Hanoi, French Indo-China.

With the exception of the one small bag containing gifts and other things for you, we sold all the personal effects of John Donovan. According to John's will, his estate was left in the care of Bob Prescott. I made the inventory with Bob and handled the auction of John's effects, after which time I left the complete care and execution of the estate in the hands of Bob Prescott. I heard from a friend at Washington that Bob has already landed in the U.S. (he was in Washington a short time ago) and according to discussions with him, he intends to see you very shortly. He has the bag containing all the effects which John wanted sent home to you.

At his death John was in possession of several Bonds on the Bank of China. These were not redeemable at the Bank of China in Kunming but would mature in several months. So I gave them to Bob Prescott, and he is returning them to you.

They can be deposited or redeemed at the Bank of China, New York, in the near future.

In regard to conditions after the war, I can hardly assure you that we shall be able to find John's grave. That depends upon the future. However, I intend to be in the Orient for the duration and perhaps longer, and want you to know that I shall, personally, do everything to establish this matter.

I am joining the Army in September and hope to be on my way back to China at the end of October.

Let me know if I can help you further.

Respectfully,
Paul Frillman
601 North Ninth
Maywood, Ill.

"He performed the impossible."

—Madame Chiang Kai-shek's final handwritten words on Chennault's honorable discharge documents for his service to China

27. AVG PASSES INTO HISTORY

On July 4, 1942, the AVG officially disbanded. They had traveled to China under a veil of secrecy and upon their disbandment there were orders for a "press blackout."

Only five pilots and 30 ground personnel chose to be inducted back into the military. Fewer than 35 of the original shark's teeth-adorned P-40Bs, Tomahawks, were still air-worthy. And 18 of the AVG pilots chose to go to work for the Chinese National Aviation Company (CNAC). Pan American Airlines and the Chinese government owned CNAC; therefore, those pilots remained civilians. The job was not hazard-free, as flying the 500-mile supply route, "The Hump," over the Himalaya mountains was extremely dangerous.

Beginning in July, Brig. General Claire Chennault commanded the newly-formed United States China Air Task Force (CATF), which included the 23rd Fighter Group with four squadrons and a bomber group. Their record was commendable, and they were credited with shooting down more than 150 Japanese planes.

Less than a year later, the CATF disbanded, and Chennault took command of the United States' 14th Air Force. This unit destroyed or damaged more than 400 Japanese planes, sank many ships, destroyed trains, trucks, and bridges while defending the Chinese from the Japanese. The record of the 14th AF is one of the most outstanding in Army Air Force history.

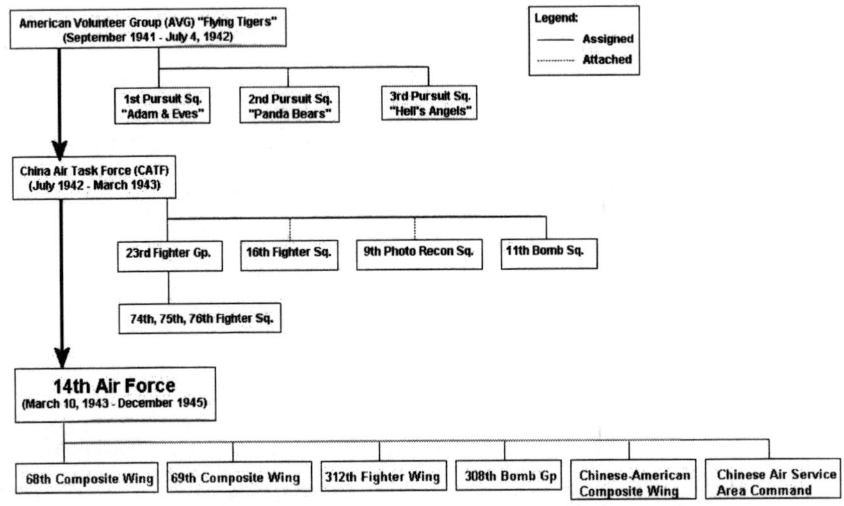

Chart courtesy of: http://www.cbi-history.com/

NEWS OF JOHN'S GRAVE IN ASSOCIATED PRESS STORY

FIGHTING FRENCHMAN WITH NEWS OF GRAVE OF JOHN DONOVAN (AP)

Chungking, October 16, 1942–(AP)

A fighting Frenchman who escaped from Japanese-occupied French Indo-China in a 14-year-old plane brought out today the first word on the fate of two American pilots of the now-dissolved AVG who were downed over the French colony.

The Americans were identified as John T. Donovan of Montgomery, Ala., killed when anti-aircraft batteries downed his plane during an AVG raid on Hanoi Airfield last May 12, and Lewis Sherman Bishop of Pensacola,

Fla., who parachuted to safety from his crippled plane near Laoka on May 17.

The Frenchman, Capt. Pierre Pouyade, said Japanese had buried Donovan without any military honors in a roadside ditch, but that during the night Frenchmen and Frenchwomen piled flowers a yard high on his grave.

Pouyade said Bishop, an AVG flight leader, was taken into custody by the French, who turned him over to the Japanese, only after the latter promised to return him. He said that was the last heard of the American.

Bishop is listed in AVG records as "to be a prisoner of war."

28. JOHN COMES HOME

Everyone who attended John's funeral in 1949 has since passed on. The cemetery caretakers and funeral home staff have, too. Memories of that day have been buried with them.

The only records that exist are the obituary clipped from the newspaper and a telegram announcing the return of John's remains with a military escort—four years after the war ended—seven years after John was shot down.

The years of effort put forth by John's mother, Stella, the U.S. government, and Graves Registration to bring John home have faded away.

What does remain is John's gravesite, his headstone, and a separate monument in his honor.

Stella, who never gave up hope and never stopped trying to bring her son home, is buried next to him. A few years following John's death she fullfilled his wishes for her to have "a more comfortable home with many flowers and trees."

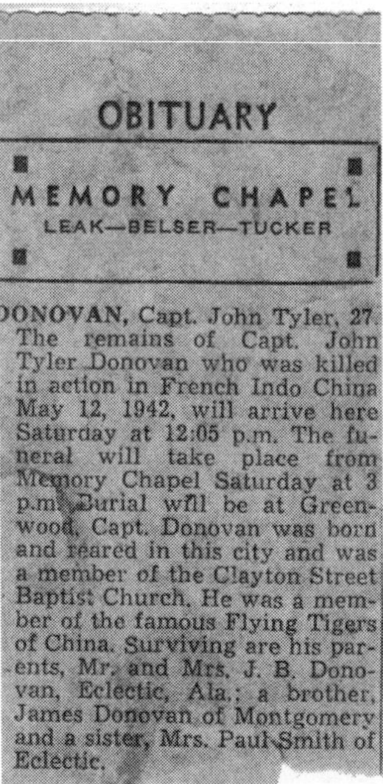

OBITUARY

MEMORY CHAPEL
LEAK—BELSER—TUCKER

DONOVAN, Capt. John Tyler, 27. The remains of Capt. John Tyler Donovan who was killed in action in French Indo China May 12, 1942, will arrive here Saturday at 12:05 p.m. The funeral will take place from Memory Chapel Saturday at 3 p.m. Burial will be at Greenwood. Capt. Donovan was born and reared in this city and was a member of the Clayton Street Baptist Church. He was a member of the famous Flying Tigers of China. Surviving are his parents, Mr. and Mrs. J. B. Donovan, Eclectic, Ala.; a brother, James Donovan of Montgomery and a sister, Mrs. Paul Smith of Eclectic.

1949 obituary

Monument in Greenwood Cemetery

Montgomery, Alabama

John Donovan's headstone in Greenwood Cemetery, Montgomery, Alabama. Photo courtesy of Kelleen Donovan Thornock

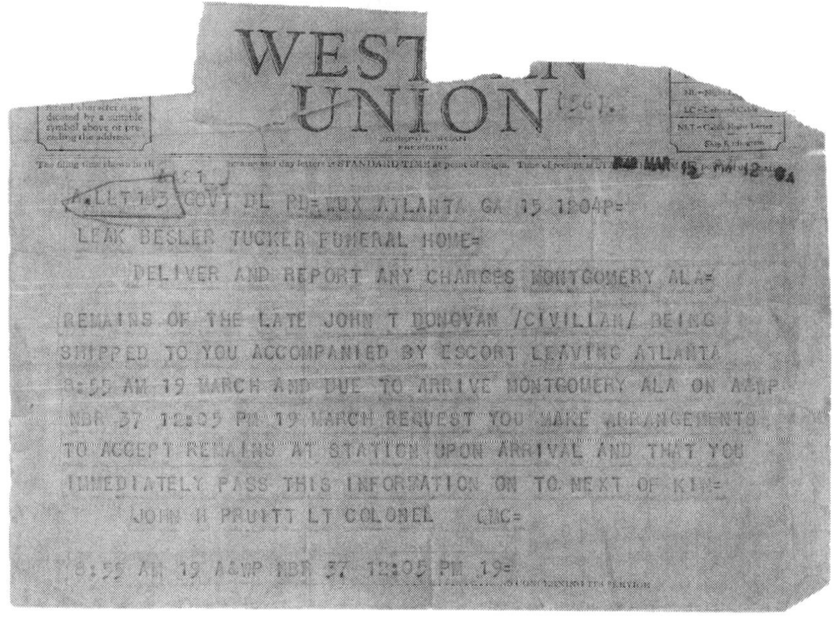

WESTERN UNION

GOVT DL PD ATLANTA GA 15 1204P=

LEAK BESLER TUCKER FUNERAL HOME=

DELIVER AND REPORT ANY CHARGES MONTGOMERY ALA=

REMAINS OF THE LATE JOHN T DONOVAN /CIVILIAN/ BEING SHIPPED TO YOU ACCOMPANIED BY ESCORT LEAVING ATLANTA 8:55 AM 19 MARCH AND DUE TO ARRIVE MONTGOMERY ALA ON A&WP NBR 37 12:05 PM 19 MARCH REQUEST YOU MAKE ARRANGEMENTS TO ACCEPT REMAINS AT STATION UPON ARRIVAL AND THAT YOU IMMEDIATELY PASS THIS INFORMATION ON TO NEXT OF KIN=

JOHN H PRUITT LT COLONEL QMC=

8:55 AM 19 A&WP NBR 37 12:05 PM 19=

This telegram was sent to the Leak Besler Tucker Funeral Home: Deliver and report any changes Montgomery Alabama

Remains of the late John T Donovan/civilian/being shipped to you accompanied by escort leaving Atlanta 8:55 a.m. 19 March and due to arrive Montgomery Ala on NBR 37 12:05 p.m. 19 March Request you make arrangements to accept remains at station upon arrival and that you immediately pass this information on to Next-Of-Kin. John H. Pruitt LT Colonel

29. UNKNOWN LEGACY

John Michael was a troubled teen in the early '50s. So troubled his mother sat him down and told him she had had enough of his behavior, and he was going away—away from the Chicago street gangs she suspected he was involved with.

Perhaps part of his problem was the lack of a father figure. Mike, as he had always been called, didn't know a lot about his father; he only knew he was dead. Now, arrangements had been made for his mother's brother in California to take him in and straighten him out.

Not surprisingly, Mike refused to leave. In the heat of the moment, his mother astonished him when she revealed that she was his grandmother. His sister, Mildred, was his real mother.

Mike did indeed go to California to live with his great uncle, who encouraged him and helped him to become the best he could be. He became a successful student and graduated on track. Mike went on to college and became a junior-high school teacher, husband, father—and a pilot like the father he never knew—John Tyler Donovan.

In the '70s, Mike's wife, Sherrie Donovan, began to research their genealogy. Naturally, she began with Mike's father. She spent hours in libraries doing research on the weekends. There was plenty of information on John Donovan and the Flying Tigers. Sherrie thought she hit the jackpot when she located Stella, Mike's paternal grandmother.

Mike wrote to Stella in 1974, but sadly she refused to believe that Mike could be John's son, saying, "John wouldn't do such a thing."

John's brother and sister, James Donovan and Mary Ellen Donovan, received letters and pictures from Mike. Without a doubt, they knew this man was their brother's son—his unknown legacy. The resemblance was uncanny. Mary Ellen and James couldn't wait to meet their "new" nephew. A part of John—regardless of the circumstances—lived on, along with Mike's three children: Mark, Jeff, and Kelleen.

After James and his wife Dorothy visited Mike for the first time, James later told me, "Finding Mike was overwhelming to me because he favored John so much in appearance and mannerism. This meeting was much like finding John alive after those many years." Jim added, "He was very much like John. Beyond appearance, he, too, had worked his way through college, loved the outdoors, and had a pilot's license."

James wondered how it was possible that John never knew about his son. "Mike explained to me that his grandmother in Chicago had intercepted all correspondence between Mildred and John, so that's why John never knew."

After a few moments Jim added, "I feel certain John would never have gone to China if he had known about Mike."

On one of their first trips to Alabama, Mary Ellen showed Kelleen a picture of John at a young age and marveled at the likeness she shared with her grandfather. She was twelve years old and remembers that occasion fondly:

"I will never forget that moment. My dad had told me stories of his father my whole life, but the moment I met the Donovans in person, I felt I became one of them. The pain of my dad never knowing his father was somehow made right in our 'adoption' into that family."

Mary Ellen removed the picture from her bedroom wall and gave it to Kelleen. For the remainder of their lives, James and Mary Ellen maintained a relationship with Mike and his children through visits, letters, and phone calls.

Stella, however, never changed her mind.

John Donovan's son, John Michael Donovan, died November 13, 1998.

1961-62

(John) Michael Donovan. Photo courtesy of Kelleen Donovan Thornock

Kelleen with her Dad Mike Donovan. Picture courtesy of Jeff Donovan

EPILOGUE

Sometime prior to 1991, long after the days of the Flying Tigers' heroics in China, documentation was submitted to the Department of the Air Force for consideration as to whether the American Volunteer Group should be considered to have served as military personnel.

The application went before the Department of Defense Civilian/ Military Service Review Board under the provision of the Department of Defense Directive 1000.20, "Active Duty Service Determination for Civilian or Contractual Groups."

All AVG personnel who were given an honorable discharge upon disbandment in July of 1942 were, without a doubt, under the direct command of a U.S. military officer, General Claire Chennault. The application was meticulously scrutinized. Here are excerpts from the board's findings:

President Roosevelt knew that the war with Japan was inevitable. The AVG was specifically created by the President to establish air bases within bombing range of Japan on China's friendly soil.

The board determined that the U.S. Armed Forces exerted control as if the group's members were military personnel from the outset of the Unites States' entry into World War II, although this control was transitioning from covert to overt until April 1942.

Although the establishment of the AVG was undertaken independently of the United States' government, members of the Roosevelt

Administration, including the President himself, as well as Secretary of the Navy Frank Cox and Secretary of the Treasury Henry Morgenthau, and others, played important roles in establishing the unit prior to Pearl Harbor. In fact, Secretary Morgenthau and other key officials arranged for the U.S. loan to the Chinese government that paid for the CAMCO contract. Furthermore, the lend-lease program was used to obtain the aircraft required by the AVG.

Signed May 3, 1991, the recommendation of the Department of Civilian/Military Service Review Board stated:

"…the service of the group known as the "Honorable discharged members of the American Volunteer Group (Flying Tigers), who served during the period December 7, 1941 to July 18, 1942, shall be considered active duty for the purposes of all laws administered by the Department of Veterans Affairs."

Obtaining military status provided services from the Veterans Administration and burial in a national cemetery. No death benefits were paid to the families of the AVG who were killed in action, including John Donovan's family.

Pilots of the AVG were awarded the Distinguished Flying Cross following this determination, and all ground personnel were awarded the Bronze Star.

This decision came 50 years after the war. Many members of the AVG had already died. John's mother, Stella, had been deceased more than 10 years. James Donovan accepted the Distinguished Flying Cross award on John's behalf in December 1996.

Today, John's granddaughter, Kelleen Donovan Thornock, proudly displays her grandfather's framed medal and citation in her home.

THE UNITED STATES OF AMERICA

TO ALL WHO SHALL SEE THESE PRESENTS, GREETING:

THIS IS TO CERTIFY THAT
THE PRESIDENT OF THE UNITED STATES OF AMERICA
AUTHORIZED BY ACT OF CONGRESS JULY 2, 1926
HAS AWARDED

THE DISTINGUISHED FLYING CROSS

TO

JOHN TYLER DONOVAN
FOR
EXTRAORDINARY ACHIEVEMENT
WHILE PARTICIPATING IN AERIAL FLIGHT
7 DECEMBER 1941 TO 18 JULY 1942

GIVEN UNDER MY HAND IN THE CITY OF WASHINGTON
THIS 8TH DAY OF DECEMBER 19 96

CHIEF OF STAFF

SECRETARY OF THE AIR FORCE

Image courtesy of Kelleen Donovan Thornock

CITATION TO ACCOMPANY THE AWARD
OF THE DISTINGUISHED FLYING CROSS (POSTHUMOUS)
TO JOHN TYLER DONOVAN

John Tyler Donovan distinguished himself by extraordinary achievement while participating in aerial flight in the South China and Southeast Asia Theater, from 7 December 1941, to 18 July 1942. The American Volunteer Group, the Flying Tigers, compiled an unparalleled combat record under extremely hazardous conditions. This volunteer unit conducted aggressive counter-air, air defense, and close air support operations against a numerically superior enemy force occasionally 20 times larger. Members of the All Volunteer Group destroyed some 650 enemy aircraft while suffering minimal losses. Their extraordinary performance in the face of seemingly overwhelming odds was a major factor in defeating the enemy's invasion of South China. The professional competence, aerial skill, and devotion to duty displayed by John Tyler Donovan reflect great credit upon himself and the Armed Forces of the United States.

GLOSSARY

Aerodrome or airdrome: British word for an airfield from which aircraft flight operations takes place.

Aileron: a hinged surface in the trailing edge of an airplane wing, used to control lateral balance.

Altitude requiring oxygen: 12,000 feet.

AVG: American Volunteer Group.

Bandoeng: A city in Indonesia now called Bandung.

Blenheim: A British mid-wing monoplane with bomb load capacity of 1,000 pounds. Top speed was 295 mph.

Brewsters: American fighter aircraft (Brewster F2A Buffalo) used by U.S. and British forces early in the war. Top speed of 327 mph.

Burma: A republic in Southeast Asia. Now called Myanmar, however, some in Burma still refuse to call it Myanmar.

By the Skin of My Teeth: Expression is as old as the Bible: From Job 19:20, King James Version, "My bone cleaveth to my skin and to my flesh, and I am escaped with the skin of my teeth." Modern usage would describe a situation of just barely getting by or narrowly escaping.

CAMCO: Central Aircraft Manufacturing Company started by William Pawley in 1933. Began doing business with Curtis-Wright, maker of the P-40s flown by AVG. Pawley worked closely with Chennault during the AVG era in China. The men recruited to fly for Chennault in 1941 were contracted though CAMCO for one year. Pawley and two brothers opened assembly plants in China for the P-40s. He later went on to become ambassador to Peru.

CATF: China Air Task Force unit replaced the Flying Tigers; however, only six pilots from the original Flying Tigers flew with this unit.

CNAC: China National Aviation Corporation conducted the first transport flights over the highest mountain range in the world, the Himalayas, better known as flying "The Hump." CNAC was the result of a cooperative venture between Pan American Airways and the government of China. In 1942, when the AVG disbanded, 17 AVG pilots chose to go to work for CNAC. Between '42 and the end of the war, CNAC flew 38,000 missions over the 500-mile Hump. Worked side by side with the 10th Air Force, providing much-needed supplies to the Allied forces.

Coolie: 19th and 20th century slang for unskilled laborers in Southern China.

Cost-like-the-deuce: A phrase similar to "hurts like the Dickens."

Croesus: Wealthy Turkish king in 560 B.C.

Curtis P-40 Aircraft: Tomahawk, Kittyhawk, and Warhawk all developed from the P-36 Hawk.
6.50-cal. machine guns
Max speed 362 MPH
Cruising speed 235 MPH
800-mile range
Length 31feet, 4 inches
Height 12 feet, 4 inches

Dottie Lamour: Dorothy Lamour, sexy Hollywood star famous for the "Road to…," a series of films with Bob Hope and Bing Crosby in the early '40s.

Dunkirk, France: Previously spelled Dunkerque in John's letters.

Dutch-mommas: Fabric-covered pillows placed between the legs on a hot night to absorb perspiration.

General Brett: Brett was Deputy Commander of the American-British-

Dutch-Australian Command (ABDACOM), which oversaw Allied forces in South East Asia and the South West Pacific.

Gun–camera: A camera attached to guns on war planes that began filming when the weapons fired. The uses were twofold: training purposes and public relations.

Gun-whales: Upper edge of the side of a vessel.

Immelmann: Aerial tactical maneuver used in dog-fights, credited to World War I German ace Max Immelmann. Not to be confused with the modern aerobatic maneuver also known as roll-off-the-top (a climbing half loop with a half-roll at the top). In a combat maneuver, after making a high-speed dive attack on the enemy, the attacker climbs back up past the enemy aircraft and, just short of a stall, applies full rudder to yaw his aircraft around. This put his aircraft facing down at the enemy making another high-speed diving pass possible. The modern term is a hammerhead turn. Illustration of the historical maneuver from a 1918 flight manual:

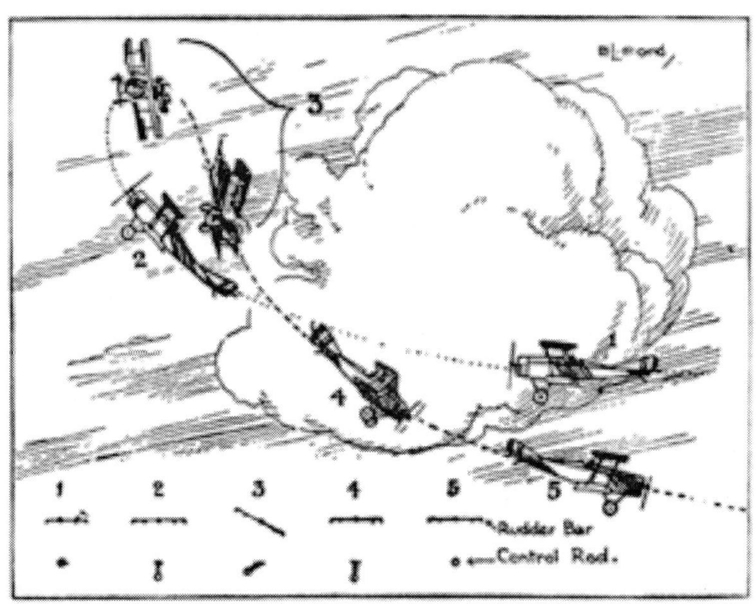

Javanese: The largest ethnic group of Indonesians on the island of Java in 1941.

Jing-baw: Air-raid.

Lend-lease: The Lend-Lease Act of March 11, 1941, was the principal means for providing U.S. military aid to foreign nations during World War II. The act authorized President Roosevelt to transfer arms and/or any other defense materials for which Congress appropriated money to "the government of any country whose defense the President deems vital to the defense of the United States." Britain, the Soviet Union, Brazil, China, and many other countries received weapons under this law.

Man-of-war: Term used for an armed vessel.

Morse code: An international method of transmitting words in a series of tones, lights, or clicks.

Moslem: Muslim. Two spellings for the same word.

NAS: Naval Air Station.

Nate: Kakajima Ki27 Japanese fighter plane.

Net: An alarm system with radios manned from the border to alert the AVG.

NJ: North American Trainer two-seat advanced training plane.

Oscar: Kakajima Ki-43 Japanese fighter plane.

Olyn Gragg: Montgomery friend who graduated from high school with John Donovan.

Pies: A pie was a unit of currency in India that is no longer in use. The smallest currency unit, equal to 1/3 paisa, 1/12 anna, or 1/192 rupee.

Pillboxes: Small bunkers that usually housed defense machine guns.

Potez 25: Twin seat, single engine French biplane with lower wing significantly smaller.

Prestone Pipe: Coolant hose on engine in P-40 Allison engine.

RAF: British Royal Air Force.

Taxi Dance Hall: A type of dance hall where dancers are paid to dance with patrons. The male patron would purchase one ticket per dance.

Tommies: British soldiers.

Trachoma: Bacterial eye infection.

Wag: Slang term for gossipers.

Wavell, Archibald Percival: 1st Earl Wavell, Commander for ABDACOM, American-British-Dutch-Australian Command. Also served as Viceroy and Governor of India.

APPENDIX

THE DISTINGUISHED FLYING CROSS MEDAL

The Cross consists of a 1½ inch cross patee. Superimposed is a four-bladed propeller, which projects slightly beyond the ends of the cross. In the angles of the cross are five sunrays that form a square, which typifies the glory and splendor of the deed for which the Cross is awarded. The medal is suspended from a red, white, and blue ribbon.

The cross symbolizes sacrifice, and the propeller symbolizes flight. The combination of those symbols makes it clear that the DFC is an award for heroism or achievement for individuals involved in aviation. The ribbon reflects the nation's colors.

[illegible], Burma Dec. 10

Dearest Folks,

The complexion of world events has taken a change and now that the U.S. is at war I hope that there will be no undue hardships on any of you. What is James doing now? I wish that he was employed in some defense job that will free him from the responsibility of joining the Army or Navy.

Over here all of us are well and happy as could be sonsidering that we are so far from home. We are well trained and able to give good account of ourselves when the time comes. You need have no worry about me as compared to the natives around here we live like Kings and have plenty of servants who call us "Mawster" and "Sahib". Our position is much less dangerous now that the Japanese have scattered their forces from the shores of America to Siam.

I have written a couple of checks totaling about 200 dollars or more on the Union Bank. These were for some jewelry and cashmere silk which I wish to bring back as presents. One of the boys was scheduled to leave yesterday from Rangoon to go back to the States and he had the package with him. Now that the war is in the Pacific, I imagine he will be back up here with us in a few days. So I will keep the stuff until I find some other way or come back myself. There was a beautiful sapphire and zircon bracelet and sapphire and diamond ring along with some hand embroidered cashmere pieces including a bedspread and table cover for you - also something nice for Mary Ellen.

We manage to get the Singapore and London radio stations as well as some in China, but not yet have we heard any news from any station in the States. I imagine the attack by the Japs rather startled everyone to say the least. I know that it is easy for the U.S. to overestimate their own state of preparedness. They are fighting a determined and resourceful enemy who is well versed in all the methods of modern warfare. We underrated the Japs and they pulled a fast one. I am convineed that they will have to pay dearly in the long run, but in the meantime they have caused considerable damage which could have been entirely avoided had we been more positive with them and less lenient.

I do not say the Japs do not have causes for their aggression; but I do say that these causes are not sufficient and for their thinking so they will bloody well find out how wrong they were.

When and if this letter reaches you is doubtful. I believe that it will, but will probably take more time than heretofore.

In my last letter I suggested some things to do with the funds in our account. These were just suggestions, if you have any need for the money other than what was suggested, then use it for whatever you please. If you don't, then I think that the bank and Federal Savings Bonds are the best things. For myself I am still getting along OK on the 75 dollars a month, but for things to bring back I will have to write checks on the checking account - for this reason, I think that it is a good idea to keep at least 500 dollars balance in this account at the Union Bank.

So far I have received only one letter from you. That means that I was here almost one month before hearing from you'all. You should not have waited so long to let me receive word as I was worried. Your letter was mailed in Montgomery about Oct. 4, I believe, and arrived here about Dec. 6. Air mail is about the only satisfactory means of writing.

We are taking it pretty easy to-day.

One of John's letters shows censoring. National Naval Aviation Museum collection

DEPARTMENT OF THE AIR FORCE
WASHINGTON DC 20330–1000

OFFICE OF THE ASSISTANT SECRETARY

19 APR 1991

MEMORANDUM FOR SAF/MI
THRU SAF/MIR

SUBJECT: Department of Defense Civilian/Military Service Review Board Recommendation on "Honorably Discharged Members of the American Volunteer Group (Flying Tigers) Who Served During the Period December 7, 1941, to July 4, 1942"

Under the provisions of DODD 1000.20, "Active Duty Service Determinations for Civilian or Contractual Groups," the Department of Defense Civilian/Military Service Review Board has considered the service of the members of the group known as "Honorably Discharged Members of the American Volunteer Group (Flying Tigers) Who Served During the Period December 7, 1941, to July 4, 1942," and has determined that the service of the group should be considered active duty for purposes of all laws administered by the Department of Veterans Affairs (VA). However, the Board determined that the cutoff date for the group is more accurately described as July 18, 1942, vice July 4, 1942.

The American Volunteer Group (AVG), was created in the summer of 1941 as an element of the Chinese Air Force to aid in the war against Japan. According to the applicant, the AVG consisted of approximately 100 pilots and another 150 personnel who were mechanics, crew chiefs, engineers, clerks, propeller specialists, parachute riggers, communications experts, armorers, doctors, and nurses. The applicant explains that "practically all" of the group's pilots and group personnel were recruited from U.S. Armed Forces. The group was commanded by retired U.S. Army Air Corps Captain Claire Lee Chennault who, prior to the creation of the AVG, was a civilian air advisor to China.

Technically, AVG personnel were under contract with a U.S. firm, the Central Aircraft Manufacturing Company (CAMCO), which in turn was under contract with the Chinese government. As U.S. Air Force historical reports explain:

> "Although the establishment of the AVG was undertaken independently of the United States government, members of the Roosevelt Administration, including the President himself, as well as Secretary of the Navy Frank Knox and Secretary of the Treasury Henry Morgenthau and others, played important roles in establishing the unit prior to Pearl Harbor. In fact, Secretary Morgenthau and other key officials arranged for the U.S. loan to the Chinese government that paid for the CAMCO contract. Furthermore, the Lend-Lease program was used to obtain the aircraft required by the AVG."

The applicant concludes from these "important roles" played by members of the U.S. government that the AVG was actually "...America's first Asian covert military operation of World War II," highlighting the fact that "In 1940, the U.S. had in operation the Neutrality Act forbidding military involvement in countries such as China." The applicant submits excerpts from an originally "Secret" 1944 Tenth Air Force historical study which explained that "...to avoid a breach of international law the entire project was organized as a commercial venture."

Armed with this background, the Board examined the applicant group against the relevant criteria. Determinations of active military service such as these are made on the extent to which civilian groups were under the control of U.S. Armed Forces in support of a military operation or mission during an armed conflict (DODD 1000.20, para D.2). The Board determined that U.S. Armed Forces exerted control as if the group's members were military personnel from the outset of the United States entry into World War II, although this control was transitioning from covert to overt until April 1942.

There is no doubt U.S. military command and control over the AVG existed when Claire Chennault was returned to active duty on April 7, 1942. At this point, the AVG was under direct command of a U.S. military officer who in turn reported directly to General Joseph W. Stilwell, commander of all American forces in India, Burma, and China. However, official U.S. Air Force history indicates that U.S. military control over the AVG actually began with the establishment of the American Military Mission to China (AMMISCA) in the fall of 1941. At this point, according to a recent report by the Office of Air Force History:

> "...the influence of U.S. military authorities over the activities and operations of the unit was extensive. In fact, in October 1941, Generalissimo Chiang Kai-shek proposed that the AMMISCA 'assume control and develop the AVG, even at the cost of separating it from the Chinese Air Force.' (Stilwell's Mission To China, p. 38). Although the AVG's absorption by the U.S. did not occur until the summer of 1942, American direction was a major factor, especially when Colonel Chennault was returned to active duty.... That action solidified U.S. military authority over the AVG. Noting Chennault's return to active duty, the Air Force's official history states: 'The AVG for all practical purposes had long since become a part of the armed forces of the United States, and plans had been made for its incorporation into the AAF (Army Air Forces).' (Plans and Early Operations p. 490.)"

The Board selected July 18, 1942, as the cutoff date for the group despite the fact that, officially, the group ceased to exist on July 4, 1942. In reality, the planned U.S. transformation of the AVG to the 23rd Pursuit Group was behind schedule and Chennault, by then a brigadier general, asked for volunteers to serve an additional two weeks. The applicant identifies 20 pilots and 24 ground personnel who accepted General Chennault's request. Two volunteer pilots were killed during the period.

Unlike the circumstances of some applicant groups, there is no doubt the AVG's service was unique. This is an important consideration since civilian service during a period of armed conflict is not necessarily equivalent to active military service, even when performed in a combat zone. Service must be beyond that generally performed by civilian employees and must be occasioned by unique circumstances. The group must have either been created to fill a wartime need or, if it existed before that time, had its prewar character substantially altered by its wartime mission. If the application is based on service in a combat zone, the mission of the group in the combat zone must have been substantially different from the mission of similar groups not in a combat zone.

The Board concluded the AVG was created to fill a wartime need, albeit initially in direct support of the Chinese since the U.S. had not entered the war. However, military histories indicate that while "...the need for protection of the Burma Road gave validity to his (Chennault's) case...the opportunity for gaining valuable combat experience against Japanese-type aircraft was an especially persuasive consideration." Further, military records show that authorization to "induct" the AVG into the U.S. Armed Forces was given immediately after Pearl Harbor, indicating plans had existed early on in the AVG's conception to eventually transform the AVG into a U.S. military unit. In summary, such documentation tends to support the applicant's conclusion that "The AVG was specifically created to circumvent existing neutrality laws that prohibited the U.S. at that time from direct military involvement. President Roosevelt knew that war with Japan was inevitable. The AVG was specifically created by the President to establish air bases within bombing range of Japan on China's friendly soil."

The Board then examined the military organizational authority over the AVG, since the concept of military control is reinforced if the military command authority determines such things as the structure of the organization, the location of the group, the mission and activities of the group, and the staffing requirements to include the length of employment and pay grades of the group. After the outbreak of the war, records show that the American Military Mission to China's "...influence...over the activities and operations of the unit was extensive." It seems reasonable to conclude that the structure of the group and its staffing requirements were driven by the number of aircraft provided to the AVG through the Lend-Lease and by U.S. intent to convert the AVG eventually into a U.S. military organization. Further, even without specific U.S. guidance, it would have been reasonable to assume that Chennault would organize the AVG according to U.S. military tradition. The contractual agreement (pay and tour of duty) between the AVG members and CAMCO may very well have been affected by the U.S. Armed Forces insofar as the President, the Secretary of the Navy, and the Secretary of the Treasury "...played important roles in establishing the unit prior to Pearl Harbor."

The Board examined next the extent of AVG integration into the U.S. military organization. Integrated civilian groups are subject to the regulations, standards, and control of the military command authority. The influence of the American Military Mission to China prior to Chennault's recall to active duty has already been discussed. Otherwise, the AVG gave the impression that members of the group were military except that they were paid and accounted for as civilians: they exchanged military courtesies (on a somewhat relaxed basis), and they wore military clothing, insignia, and devices. Finally, integration into the military may lead to an expectation by members of the group that the service of the group imminently would be recognized as active military service. Such integration acts in favor of recognition, and documents show that the pilots recruited for the AVG were promised that time spent in the AVG would count toward promotion upon their guaranteed reentry into the U.S. armed forces.

Next, the Board considered whether the AVG was subject to military discipline since civilians are sometimes restricted as if they were military members. The applicant's interviews with former members of the AVG indicate that after December 7, 1941, Chennault imposed a general curfew requiring all AVG personnel to be on base, required specific passes to travel from the base's proximity and put all three AVG squadrons on 24-hour alert. Chennault instituted special discipline boards which fined members for certain transgressions such as failure to stay in proper physical condition or absence without leave (AWOL). Further, the contract signed by AVG personnel explained that they could be fired for insubordination, revealing confidential information, habitual use of drugs, excessive use of alcohol, illness or disability incurred due to a member's own misconduct, and malingering. Finally, after Pearl Harbor, Chennault fired 10 pilots and 37 ground personnel for various misconduct by giving them "dishonorable discharges." This application is filed only on behalf of those AVG personnel discharged with honorable discharges.

The Board likewise considered whether AVG personnel were subject to military justice. While there is no record of U.S. military judicial proceedings involving AVG personnel, the lack of serious crimes combined with Chennault's system of dishonorable discharges may have precluded courts-martial action.

The Board also considered whether any prohibition existed to prohibit members of the group from joining the armed forces. That is, some organizations may be formed to overcome existing laws or treaties or because of a governmentally-established policy to retain individuals in the group as part of a civilian force. Such factors act in favor of recognition. The AVG, in fact, was apparently formed as a civilian force to overcome existing neutrality law. Thus, members of the AVG were prohibited from remaining with, as opposed to "not joining," the U.S. Armed Forces.

The Board then considered whether the AVG employed skills or resources that were enhanced as the result of military training or equipment designed or issued to achieve a military capability. In the case of the AVG, they were recruited because of military training they already possessed and they employed equipment provided to the Chinese through the Lend-Lease program. Thus, the Board felt the AVG satisfied this criteria.

The Board was also compelled to consider whether the AVG satisfied certain criteria which do not favor recognition. First, the Board easily dismissed the possibility that the AVG submitted itself to the U.S. Armed Forces for protection. In this case, the AVG provided protection to U.S. and Allied forces. Since the ability of personnel to resign at will and without penalty indicates a lack of military control, the Board examined this factor. Here the applicant submitted as evidence the diary records of a former AVG member who claimed that Chennault informed AVG personnel on April 19, 1942, that anyone "resigning voluntarily would be guilty of desertion." Records indicate that Chennault issued dishonorable discharges for desertion although evidence is not clear if the desertion was in the form of such "voluntary resignations." AVG personnel signed contracts of one year duration and the contracts did not address voluntary resignations during the one year period. However, a memorandum to Secretary Knox shows that prior to May 20, 1942, Chennault requested the War Department to "prevent personnel deserting AVG and getting back to the United States via Army ferry planes from India." Thus, the lack of transportation may have been a practical obstacle to resignation. Finally, the Board noted that the applicant was claiming no prior Federal or state recognition as a basis for recognition under DODD 1000.20.

In addition to other factors, the Board also considered the status of the AVG in international law. That is, were members of the group regarded and treated as civilians, or assimilated into the Armed Forces as reflected in treaties, customary international law, judicial decisions, and U.S. diplomatic practice? The Board concluded that members of the AVG were considered combatants and were entitled to, and accorded, prisoner of war status. Further, the Board concluded that AVG members were not merely "assimilated to the armed forces" but rather were an armed force.

Therefore, all criteria considered, the Board recommends the Secretary sign the attached instrument determining that the service of this group, as defined by the Board, be considered active duty for the purposes of all laws administered by the Department of Veterans Affairs.

ELLWOOD P. HINMAN III
Brigadier General, USAF
President
DOD Civilian/Military
Service Review Board

1 Attachment
Secretarial Instrument

DEPARTMENT OF THE AIR FORCE
WASHINGTON DC 20330-1000

OFFICE OF THE ASSISTANT SECRETARY

Upon the recommendation of the Department of Defense Civilian/Military Service Review Board, the service of the group known as the "Honorably Discharged Members of the American Volunteer Group (Flying Tigers) Who Served During the Period December 7, 1941 to July 18, 1942" shall be considered active duty for the purposes of all laws administered by the Department of Veterans Affairs.

To receive recognition, each applicant must meet the following eligibility criteria:

Must have served honorably with the AVG in China during the period beginning December 7, 1941 through July 17, 1942 as evidenced by:

a. An AVG Honorable discharge certificate or letter

or

b. Identification as an Honorably discharged AVG member in other credible publications or documents.

3 May 91
(Date)

J. G. COOPER
Assistant Secretary of the Air Force
(Manpower, Reserve Affairs, Installations and Environment)

7

CONFIDENTIAL

DRO:cn

(1-A)

MEMORANDUM for: The Chief of Staff. March 29, 1941

SUBJECT: Pilots for the Chinese Air Force.

1. A representative of this office attended a meeting in the office of Captain M.L. Deyo, Assistant to The Secretary of Navy, March 28, 1941, for the purpose of securing information relative to the plans that have been made to furnish 100 reserve officer pilots for the Chinese Air Force.

2. Final negotiations with the Chinese Government have not been completed, but it is contemplated that the reserve officers, after resigning their commissions, will be given contracts with the Central Aircraft Company, an American firm located in China. This company is owned by the Curtiss-Wright Corporation and the Inter-Continental Company of China. At the present time, the Curtiss-Wright Corporation has controlling interest. The pilots will be paid by this concern and will have no financial dealings whatsoever with the Chinese Government. Contracts are to extend for one year.

3. The Navy Department has adopted the following plan to secure volunteers for this duty:

a. Mr. Leighton of the Central Aircraft Company and Captain Claire Chennault, U.S.A.Retired, will be furnished letters of introduction to the Commandant of Naval Air Stations.

b. Confidential letters will be sent to Station Commanders outlining in brief the reason for the visit and authorizing reserve officers to volunteer for this service.

c. Mr. Leighton and Captain Chennault will be allowed to visit any of the Naval Air Stations and explain their proposition to the naval reserve officers.

d. Volunteers will submit their resignations direct to Captain M.L. Deyo, Assistant to The Secretary of Navy. Resignations will be accepted "without prejudice", which means that they may be reinstated in the naval reserve after completion of their contract and the year's absence will be considered as a year of duty as far as promotion is concerned.

4. No mention was made in the meeting reference the number of officers to be furnished by either the Army or Navy.

5. Any specific amount of flying experience was not discussed. It is known that the Chinese mission particularly desires pilots who have had experience in flying the P-40 type airplane. They are well aware of the fact that it is doubtful if this can be done and contemplate holding approximately ten of their P-40 airplanes in this country for the purpose of giving transition flying to volunteers. This flying will be conducted at some civil airport.

(47) AG 320.18 (3-29-41)

CONFIDENTIAL

6. In addition to officer volunteers, the Chinese Mission will be alowed to solicity approximately 100 enlisted mechanics and clerks. Due to loss of longevity privileges for regular navy enlisted personnel who request discharge for this duty, the Navy Department contemplates restricting volunteers to their enlisted reserve.

7. Army Air Corps has been directed to adopt Navy procedure in this matters. (H.H.A.)

stamped:
H.H.Arnold,
Major General,Air Corps,
Chief of the Air Corps.

APPROVED
By order of the Secretary of War
H.H.ARNOLD
Deputy Chief of Staff

/s/ Orlando Ward

by Orlando Ward,
Lt. Col.,G.S.C.,Sec.W.D.G.S.

Original Gen S.W. by Gen Arnold
c.n.

He told me that S/W approved.
cn

C
O
P
Y

1914
I certify this is
a true copy.
JGB

J.G. Boykin
Lt. Col.
AGO

SECURITY CLASSIFICATION
REVIEWED AUTH. SEC. ARMY
By TAG per 9T-5

CONFIDENTIAL

Documents courtesy of National Archives, College Park, Maryland

3RD SQUADRON ROSTER

HONORABLY DISCHARGED JULY 4, 1942

Frank Adkins Flight Lead

Charles Baisden Armorer

Lewis Bishop Vice Squadron Lead

Robert Brouk Flight Lead

Herbert Cavanah Flight Lead

Keith Christensen Armorer

L. Paul Clouthier Clerk-Operations

Leon Colquette Crew Chief

Jesse Crookshanks Crew Chief

John Donovan Wing Man

Parker Dupouy Vice Squadron Lead

Charles Engle Crew Chief

John Fauth Crew Chief

Ben Foshee Wing Man

Charles Francisco Communications

Edward Gallagher Crew Chief

Henry Gilbert Wing Man

Paul Greene Flight Lead

Clifford Groh Flight Lead

Maax Hammer Wing Man

Thomas Haywood Flight Lead

Robert Hedman Flight Lead

Fred Hodges Flight Lead

Daniel Hoyle Clerk-Admin

Kenneth Jernstedt Flight Lead

Thomas Jones Vice Squadron Lead

Daniel Keller Crew Chief

George Kepka Crew Chief

C.H. Link Laughlin Flight Lead

Elton Loomis Communications
Frank Losonsky Crew Chief
Lacy Mangleburg Wing Man
Neil Martin Flight Lead
Gale Mc Allister Crew Chief
George Mc Millan Flight Lead
Charles Older Flight Lead
Arvid Olson Squadron Lead
Henry Olson Crew Chief
Harold Osborne Crew Chief
Ed Overend Flight Lead
Paul Perry Armorer
Joseph Poshefko Armorer
Robert Raine Flight Lead
William Reed Flight Lead
Stanley Regis Crew Chief
Clarence Riffer Armorer
Leo Schramm Crew Chief
Wilfred Seiple Crew Chief
Erik Shilling Flight Lead
Robert A. Smith Crew Chief
Robert T. Smith Flight Lead
Edward Stiles Crew Chief
Irving Stolet Crew Chief
Joseph Sweeney Communications
Julian Terry Clerk-Admin
Frank Van Timmeren Line Chief

Author's Note: Only the 3rd Squadron personnel list is included because this book is about John Donovan, a member of the 3rd Squadron. By no means is this a complete book about the American Volunteer Group.

AVG PILOTS LOST

Lacy Mangleburg, Wingman, Accident, December 23, 1941
Neil Martin, Flight Lead, KIA, December 23, 1941
Henry Gilbert, Wingman, KIA, December 23, 1941
Kenneth Merritt, Wingman, Accident, January 8, 1942
Allen Christman, Flight Lead, KIA, January 23, 1942
Louis Hoffman, Flight Lead, KIA, January 26, 1942
Thomas Cole, Wingman, KIA, January 30, 1942
Robert Sandell, Squadron Leader, Accident, February 7, 1942
Edward Leibolt, Flight Lead, MIA, February 25, 1942
John Newkirk, Squadron Leader, KIA, March 24, 1942
Ben Foshee, Wingman, Died from wounds, May 4, 1942
John Donovan, Wingman, KIA, May 12, 1942
Thomas Jones, Squadron Leader, Accident, May 16, 1942
Robert Little, Flight Lead, KIA, May 22, 1942
Frank Swartz, Wingman, Died from wounds, April 24, 1942
John Blackburn, Wingman, Accident, April 26, 1942

"For every pilot the AVG lost, the Japanese lost twenty-eight."
—*Flying Tigers* by Dan Ford, p. 336

AVG CAPTURED

Flight Lead Charles Mott Captured January 8th, 1942
Liberated 1945 Died August 14, 2004 He was 89 years old

Wingman William McGarry Captured March 24, 1942
Credited with designing the 1st Squadron logo Adam & Eves
Escaped with the help of the Office of Strategic Services—
Smuggled out of Bangkok in a coffin.
Died April 1990, he was 74 years old.

Vice Squadron Leader Lewis Bishop Captured May 17, 1942.
Escaped three years later on a moving train full of Chinese prisoners who aided in his escape. Lewis Bishop, along with his daughter Sheila Bishop Irwin, wrote his memoir, *Escape from Hell: An AVG Flying Tiger's Journey.* Lewis Bishop Died November 1, 1997, at the age of 72.

SALUTE TO THE FLYING TIGERS

Speech given by Generalissimo Chiang Kai-shek at the banquet dinner in Kunming in honor of the American Volunteer Group of the Chinese Air Force.

"Colonel Chennault, officers and men: To be with you American volunteers here today, to observe your excellent spirit and to hear of your achievements, fills me with delight and admiration. The American Volunteer Group of the Chinese Air Force has acquired a world-wide reputation for greatest courage.

It is three months since the Japanese, our common enemy, picked their quarrel with Great Britain and the United States. The splendid victories the Volunteer Group has won in the air are a glory that belongs to China and our ally, America, alike.

I have already communicated the news of your repeated successes to your Government and President Roosevelt. The record of what you have done shows that every one of you has been a match for thirty or more of the enemy. Your friends and relations will undoubtedly have felt boundless pride and elation to hear of your exploits. The blows you have struck at the Japanese have put you in the forefront of the Allied forces fighting the aggressor. You have established a firm foundation for the campaign against this lawlessness which China and America are united to wage. You have written in the history of this world war a remarkable page, the memory of which will live in our minds forever…"

MADAME CHIANG'S SPEECH

"Colonel Chennault, members of the A.V.G. and other friends: As your Honorary Commander, may I call you my boys? You have flown across the Pacific in China's gravest hour on wings of hope and faith. For this reason not only do the Chinese Air Force but the entire Chinese nation welcome you with outstretched arms. The Generalissimo has already spoken to you of the fine and brave deeds you have done, and he has called the A.V.G. the world's bravest air force.

I am very proud tonight that I have had a little share in making it possible for you to fight for China. When I think of the life-and-death struggle which China has passed through these last five years, I have before my mind's eye the millions of our people who have been killed or wounded and others who had to flee from Japanese cannon, machine-guns and bombers. I also see the rivers of blood, which have flowed over our territory, the very life-blood of China's fairest manhood. I think of the tens of thousands of our women whose honor has been violated by the Japanese, and the hundreds of thousands of our little children who have been killed and maimed, or else taken to Japan to be trained as traitors to their motherland.

And now you have come here to vindicate us. We have always been resolved to fight until final victory is ours, but we lack the air arms, which you are now providing. You have come to fight side by side with us. For this I wish to express our heartfelt thanks.

Colonel Chennault has taken an active part in Chinese resistance during the last five years. You boys know him personally. You know what an admirable commander he is and how very selfless. The only complaint I have against him is that he is never satisfied with his own work. I venture to say, too, that he also thinks that you ought to have more work regardless of how much you already have.

Colonel Chennault has just introduced me as Honorary Commander of the A.V.G. I think I am prouder of this title than of any other title I've had because I know that you are not only fighting with your bodies and your skill, you are fighting with your hearts and spirits. Just now Colonel Chennault brought to me two of your very fine comrades who have braved death to-day in the air. They forgot themselves entirely while fighting the enemy because they know that although they might have to make the final sacrifice, their comrades would carry on the great work which the A.V.G. has set for itself. This spirit, I feel, is the secret of the A.V.G.'s successes.

I was asked a little while ago by one of my officers: "Madame Chiang, some of the A.V.G. pilots are shooting down so many planes that we won't have room enough on the wings for all the stars which they merit. What shall we do about it ?" I told him: "We shall have to provide them with an additional pair of wings." And that is what we will have to do if you all keep up the score. Although you are here in China I am sure that often your minds and your hearts fly back to your loved ones in America, and for this reason I am glad that America is now realizing that China is not fighting for China alone, but for America and for the whole world. You, in giving the best that is in you, are doing it for your own country as well as for China. Time and again your Commanding Officer has dinned into your ears the necessity for discipline. Hateful word, isn't it? Discipline in the air, discipline on the field, and yet without discipline we can accomplish nothing, and I, as your Honorary Commanding Officer, am going to din more discipline into you.

I would go further than Colonel Chennault. I mean the discipline of your inner selves. It isn't enough to observe discipline only. We must have inner discipline so that we may have fully developed characters. However, I am not trying to make you little prospered saints, and I am quite human to like interesting people, but I do want you boys to remember one thing: the whole of the Chinese nation has taken you to its heart, and I want you to conduct yourselves in a manner worthy of the great traditions that you have built up. I want you to leave an impression on my people, a true impress of what Americans really are. I trust and I know that you will act worthily wherever you are in China.

Forgive me for speaking to you like that. Perhaps I should be very polite and say: "Boys, you are just grand. You are little angels with or without wings." But you are my boys. I can speak to you freely. I know that you will understand when I say that I hope every one of you, whether in the air or on the ground, will remember that you are China's guests and that everything you do will reflect credit upon the country which I love next to my own, America, where, as you know, I was educated, and which I always look upon as my second home.

Colonel Chennault just now said something which rather embarrassed me. He spoke to you about my needing money to carry on relief work. I know that money is necessary, Colonel, but I don't want to rope you boys in tonight for this purpose. If I had, this dinner would be very hard to digest, so I didn't do that, but I do want to thank you for what you voluntarily contributed to the war orphans during Christmas. Please don't feel that you have to contribute now, that's one thing I beg of you.

Just one final word. War is not only a matter of equipment, artillery, ground troops or air force; it is largely a matter of spirit, or morale. When I came into this room I felt at once how very keyed up you are. Now that you have been fighting for a few months you are full of enthusiasm and pep. That is a good thing but the greater thing is to gather momentum as each day goes by and not let yourself be discouraged, no matter what happens because as you soar into the skies you are writing in letters of flame on the horizon certain eternal truths for the world to see: first, the indomitable courage of the Chinese people; second, the indestructible spirit of the Chinese Army; and third, the deathless soul of the Chinese nation. And so, whatever you do, wherever you are, remember that such is the China which you have come to assist.

I would like all of you to get up and drink a toast to the two great sister nations of both sides of the Pacific. They now have a bond of friendship and sympathy which serves us well in the crucible of war and which will serve us equally well when victory has been won."

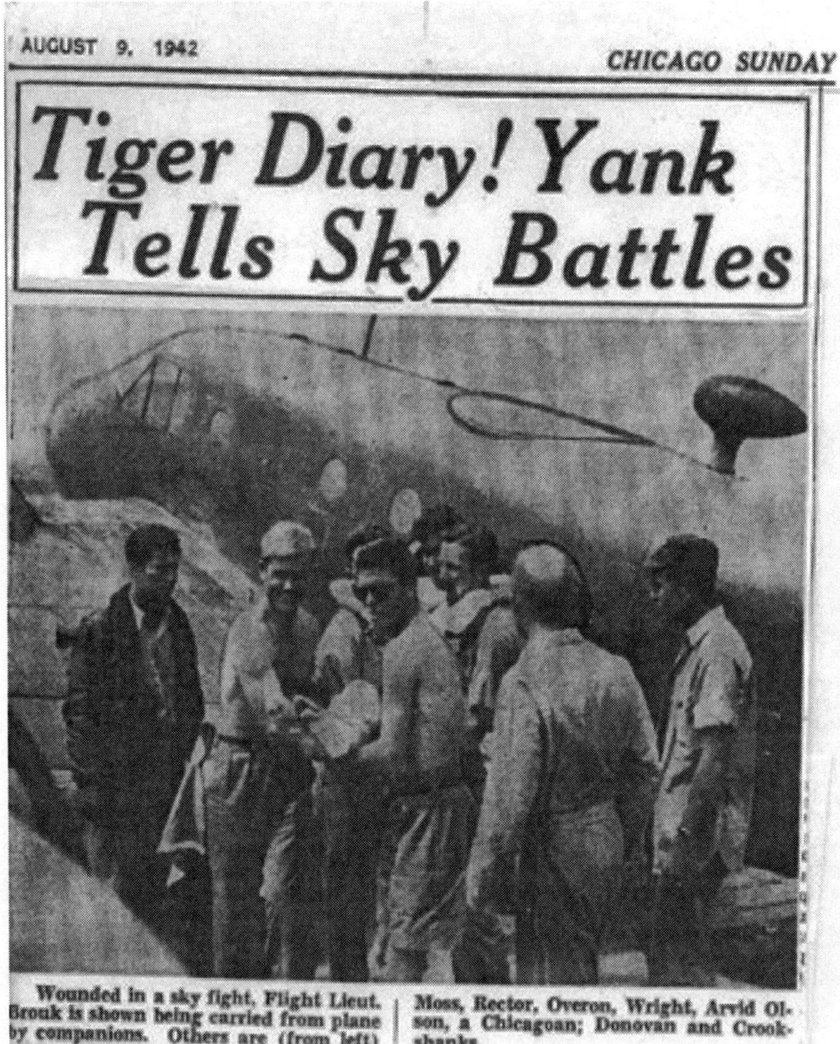

AUGUST 9, 1942 CHICAGO SUNDAY

Tiger Diary! Yank Tells Sky Battles

Wounded in a sky fight, Flight Lieut. Brouk is shown being carried from plane by companions. Others are (from left) Moss, Rector, Overon, Wright, Arvid Olson, a Chicagoan; Donovan and Crookshanks.

The date on this newspaper shows the significant time lag in writing the story to actual print time. This incident occurred on May 5, 1942. John is in the forefront with his back to the camera.

A PROUD
NATION HAILS A
GREAT FILM TRIUMPH!
FLYING
TIGERS
JOHN WAYNE
JOHN CARROLL · ANNA LEE
PAUL KELLY
GORDON JONES
MAE CLARKE
BILL SHIRLEY
THRILLING PRAISE!
It's a
REPUBLIC PICTURE

★ John Tyler Donovan, Government '40, was flight instructor at Pensacola when he resigned an ensign in the Naval Reserve last summer to join the American Volunteer Group. He has been with Colonel Chennault in Burma since September of 1941.

Clapper's Letter

By RAYMOND CLAPPER
(Distributed by United Features)

CHUNGKING, April 8 — Even the vaunted American Volunteer Group is now suffering from a shortage of planes. The AVG has been gradually whittled down, although in so doing it has established a heroic record for quantity of Japanese aircraft destroyed. The successes of the AVG are the talk of all Africa and Asia. I have heard its praises sung everywhere I have been.

[illegible]

MONTGOMERY TIGER—John Donovan, one of General Chennault's Flying Tigers of the American Volunteer Group, stands in front of one of the P-40's which have been knocking down Jap planes at a steady rate since Pearl Harbor. The sharks teeth painted on the plane's nose is a decoration designed to increase the well-founded fears of the Japs.

Johnny Donovan Of The AVG Chalks Up Another Jap Down

[illegible]

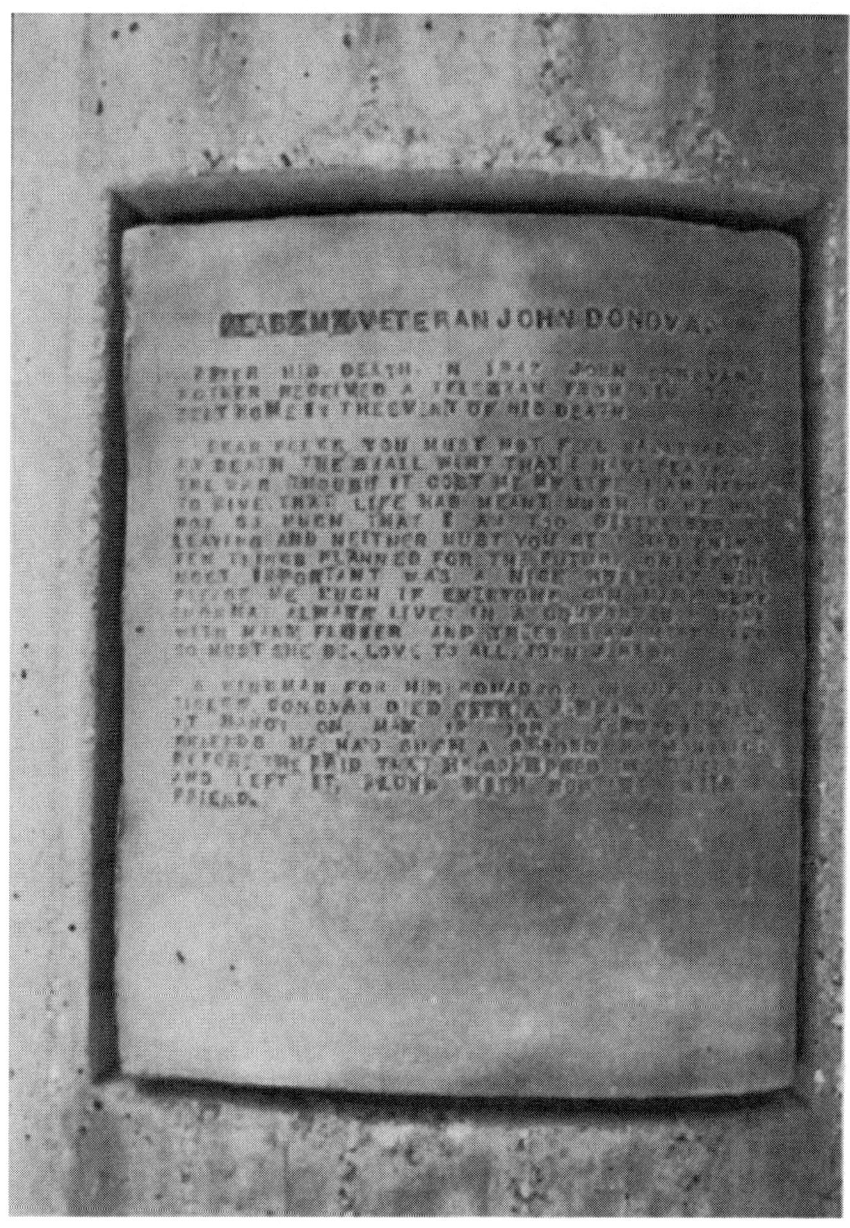

Alabama Veterans Memorial Park

100 Overton Access Road, Birmingham

Alabama Veterans Memorial Park. One pillar, permanently etched, is dedicated to John Donovan and commemorates his last words to his family.

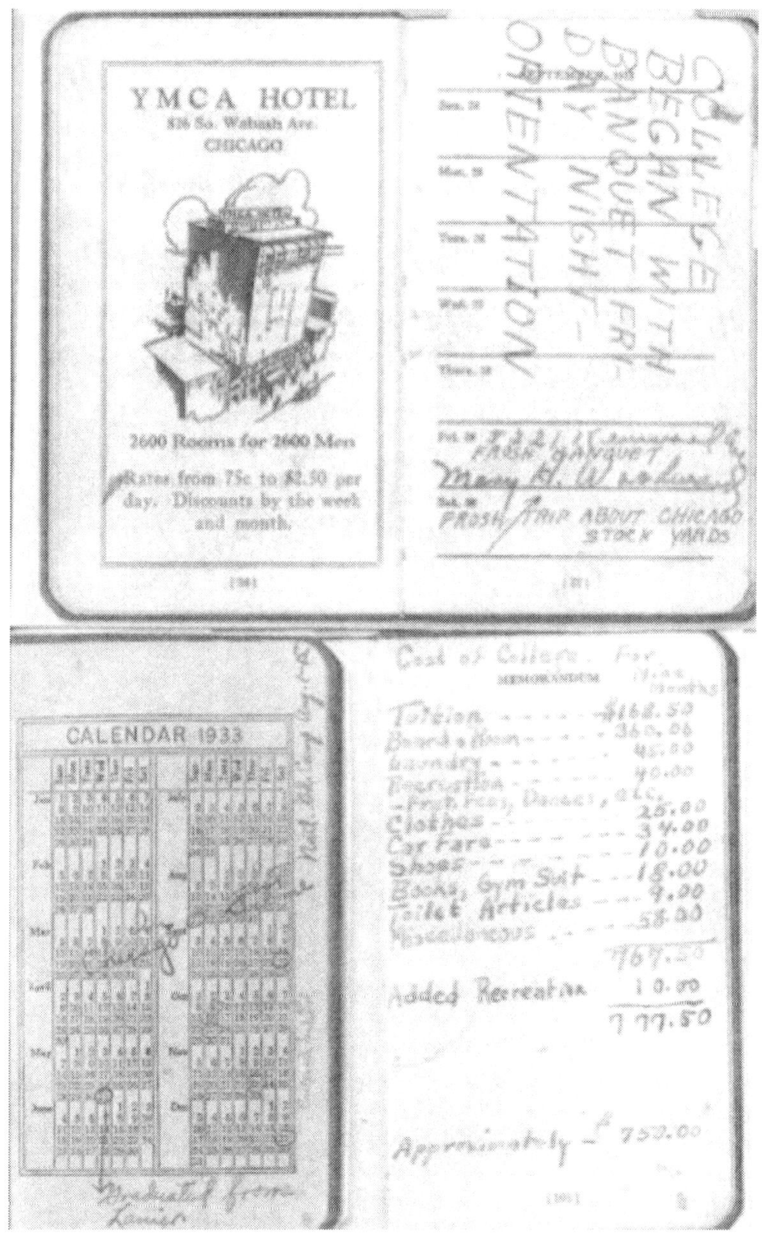

YMCA HOTEL
826 So. Wabash Ave.
CHICAGO

2600 Rooms for 2600 Men

Rates from 75c to $2.50 per day. Discounts by the week and month.

COLLEGE BEGAN WITH BANQUET FRIDAY NIGHT - ORIENTATION

FROSH BANQUET

FROSH TRIP ABOUT CHICAGO STOCK YARDS

CALENDAR 1933

Cost of College For Nine Months

MEMORANDUM

Tuition - - - - - $168.50
Board & Room - - - - 360.00
Laundry - - - - - 45.00
Recreation - - - - - 40.00
- Frat. Fees, Dances, etc. 25.00
Clothes - - - - - - 34.00
Car Fare - - - - - - 10.00
Shoes - - - - - - 18.00
Books, Gym Suit - - 9.00
Toilet Articles - - - 58.00
Miscellaneous - - -

767.50

Added Recreation 10.00

777.50

Approximately $752.00

John's 1933 diary. He worked at the YMCA to pay his college tuition.

SQUADRONS

1st Pursuit Squadron Adam and Eves

2nd Pursuit Squadron Panda Bears

3rd Squadron Hell's Angels

BIBLIOGRAPHY

Baldwin, R.E., *Last Hope: The Blood Chit Story,* Schiffer Military History, Atglen, PA, 1997

Bergin, Bob, *Tracking the Tiger: Flying Tigers, OSS and Free Thai Operations in World War II Thailand,* Banana Tree Press, Electronic Book 2011

Byrd, Martha, *Chennault: Giving Wings to the Tiger,* University of Alabama Press, 1987

Bond, Charles R., *A Flying Tiger's Diary,* Texas A & M University Press, 1984

Boyington, Greg, *Baa Baa Black Sheep,* G.P. Putnum's Sons, New York, 1958, p.23

Esposito, Brigadier General Vincent L., Chief Editor, *West Point Atlas of War World War II: The Pacific,* Tess Press, New York, 1959

Ford, Daniel, *Flying Tigers: Claire Chennault and his American Volunteers, 1941-1942,* Smithsonian Books, 2007 Revised Edition

Gamble, Bruce, *Black Sheep One,* Presidio Press, 2000, p.120

Heiferman, Ronn, *Flying Tigers: Chennault in China,* Ballantine Books, New York, 1971

Li, Laura Tyson, *Madame Chiang Kai-Shek,* Atlantic Monthly Press, New York, 2006

Lopez, Donald S., *Into the Teeth of the Tiger,* Smithsonian Books, Washington, D.C., 1997

Mims, Sam, *Chennault of the Flying Tigers,* Macrae-Smith-Company, Philadelphia, 1943

Rodger, George, Photographer, *Flying Tigers in Burma,* Life Magazine, Vol.12, No. 13, March 30, 1942

Smith, Nichol, *Burma Road,* Bobbs-Merrill Company, 1940

Smith, Robert M., *With Chennault in China: A Flying Tiger's Diary,* Tab Books, 1984

Whelan, Russell, *The Flying Tigers,* Garden City Publishing Company, Inc., 1944, p.198

ONLINE REFERENCES

https://archive.org/stream/voiceofchinaspee00chia/voiceofchinaspee00chia_djvu.txt

http://www.dfcsociety.net/the-medal/

http://www.nationalmuseum.af.mil/

http://www.zzwave.com/cmfweb/wiihist/njmassac/rape.htm

http://digitalcommons.iwu.edu/cgi/viewcontent.cgi?article=1217&context=constructing

AUTHOR'S POSTSCRIPT

Six years ago I was living in Washington State, working as a florist, and never dreamed of writing a book—much less two. Believing things happen for a reason, I have often wondered why I landed here in Georgia, much like I have every other time I landed somewhere. And I've landed in eight different states for eight different reasons.

This time, I feel in my heart it must have been for the incredible writing community I've been fortunate enough to find. I can't thank my critique group enough for their acceptance, encouragement, support, and love throughout both endeavors. Carolyn Graham, Mari Ann Stefanelli, and Jane Shirley—I treasure all of you!

Jedwin Smith, thank you for being there with answers to my many questions. Be it writing or history, or just moral support, you have always come through for me—and I thank you.

Pat Donovan Hope, Bud Hope, Wayne Smith, Kelleen Donovan Thornock, Jeff Donovan, Hill Goodspeed, Dina Linn, Rachel Sims, Alan Armstrong, Brad Smith, Bob Bergin, Albert Alyn, Nell Calloway & the entire Chennault Aviation & Military Museum staff, Redina Miller, Mike Miller, your help is immeasurable—and I know the answer from each of you could easily have been, Sorry, I don't have the time. Thank you for always finding the time for me. If I have omitted anyone, I apologize—and thank you.

To my family and friends, thank you for your support and encouragement.

To Deeds Publishing, thank you for being so pleasant to work with again. I could not ask for a more congenial working relationship.

To my editor, Mari Ann Stefanelli, thank you for your expertise and your patience. It is clear to me that editing is more than your profession—it's your calling.

And last, but certainly not least, thank you to my husband, Mike, for countless hours of quiet (yours and mine) so I could write, for not complaining when things did not get done around the house, and especially—for believing in me.

ABOUT THE AUTHOR

Susan Clotfelter Jimison, author of *Dear Mark,* lives in the Atlanta area with her husband, Mike, and the best dog in the world—Dude. Her memoir, *Dear Mark,* was nominated for the 2015 Georgia Author of the Year Award in the memoir category.

CPSIA information can be obtained at www.ICGtesting.com
Printed in the USA
LVOW06s0210011015

456162LV00004B/8/P